Wildlife Watching in America's National Parks

Wildlife Watching in America's National Parks

A SEASONAL GUIDE

Gary W. Vequist & Daniel S. Licht

TEXAS A&M UNIVERSITY PRESS ⚓ COLLEGE STATION

Library of Congress Cataloging-in-Publication Data

   Wildlife watching in America's national parks : a seasonal guide /
Gary W. Vequist and Daniel S. Licht. — 1st ed.
       p. cm.
   Includes bibliographical references and index.
   ISBN 978-1-60344-814-7 (flexbound (with flaps) : alk. paper)—
   ISBN 1-60344-814-4 (flexbound (with flaps) : alk. paper)—
   ISBN 978-1-60344-827-7 (ebook—p)—
   ISBN 1-60344-827-6 (ebook—p)
   1. Wildlife watching—United States.
2. Wildlife recovery—United States.
3. National parks and reserves—United States.
I. Licht, Daniel S., 1960-   II. Title.
   QL155.V38 2013
   590.72'34—dc23
   2012028695

*Cover photos by Daniel S. Licht (western tanager and prairie dog)
and National Park Service (sea turtle hatchlings).*

Contents

Additional Parks by Chapter

CHAPTER 1
Grand Teton National Park
North Cascades National Park and Ross Lake National Recreation Area
Voyageurs National Park
Isle Royale National Park

CHAPTER 2
Shenandoah National Park
Delaware Water Gap National Recreation Area
Yosemite National Park
Sequoia and Kings Canyon National Parks
Yellowstone National Park
Katmai National Park

CHAPTER 3
Wind Cave National Park
Devils Tower National Monument
Theodore Roosevelt National Park
Bryce Canyon National Park
Dinosaur National Monument

CHAPTER 4
Gulf Islands National Seashore
Biscayne National Park
Canaveral National Seashore
Padre Island National Seashore

CHAPTER 5
Tallgrass Prairie National Preserve
Wind Cave National Park
Badlands National Park
Yellowstone National Park

CHAPTER 6
Bandelier National Monument
Big Bend National Park

Preface

The idea for this book surfaced while observing an evening flight of bats at Carlsbad Caverns National Park, New Mexico. A small gathering of people watched in awe as wave after wave of bats exited the cave, circled overhead in the fading light, and then disappeared into the night sky. It was apparent that many of the spectators had arrived at the park only a few hours earlier, solely to tour the cave and view its geologic wonders, unaware that on this summer evening one of nature's great wildlife spectacles would occur. It was also apparent that many other park visitors, including families with children, had left the park earlier in the day and were back at their hotel rooms. They had missed a breathtaking and unforgettable wildlife-viewing experience.

Unfortunately, this pattern is played out in national parks across the country. Geysers, mountains, and caves attract the visitors in large part because they are easy to see and reliable. Yet it's the elusive wildlife that often leaves the most indelible memories. A glimpse of a wolf, the roar of the rutting bison, or the playful antics of the prairie dog are not soon forgotten. But seeing these creatures is not always easy, especially for folks who have limited outdoor experience. Therefore, we have written this book as a guide to seeing wild animals in America's national parks.

We recognize that people have busy lives and may have limited time to view wildlife, so we've identified the best places and times to see the critters. For example, spring is a great time to observe black bears at Great Smoky Mountains National Park, as the animals have just emerged from their winter slumber and are out foraging in the greening meadows. Furthermore, the crowds of people are smaller than they are in summer. We also identify times when the animals are most interesting, enhancing the observer's experience. For example, winter is one of the best times to watch bald eagles as they congregate near the open water of the Mississippi National River and Recreation Area. At this time of year visitors are assured of watching scores of eagles hunt, fight, steal prey, court, and exhibit all the other behaviors that make them so fascinating. And because no animal is an island, we discuss the other species that our focal species interact with, including species they prey on, or may be preyed by. After all, truly understanding the focal species can only be attained when visitors appreciate the intricate web of life they are a part of.

As the title implies, this is also a book about America's national parks. Our National Park System has often been described as America's best idea, and we concur. Our national parks are part of our history and, we hope, part of our future and a gift to future generations. Wildlife is an integral part of what makes these lands so priceless. There is, of course, lots of great information already available regarding our parks; however, when it comes to seeing wildlife in the parks, much of that information only scratches the surface. The existing information may give you a list of species present in a park, but we try to tell you how best to see the animals, where in the park they are, and when the best time is to see them. Furthermore, we cover the entire National Park System, giving the reader a system-wide perspective on wildlife watching. As this book demonstrates, just about every part of the country has a park unit within a short drive.[1] Readers may notice that the feature parks are all located in the lower forty-eight states. Our goal is to highlight parks and wildlife that are easily accessible to large numbers of people. There are, of course, incredible wildlife-viewing opportunities in Alaska, Hawaii, and the US territories outside the contiguous states (e.g., Virgin Islands), but space limitations allow us to mention only a few of these spectacular parks.

Although our goal is to describe wildlife watching in national parks, there is simply no way we could cover the tens of thousands of species found in the hundreds of park units. Therefore, we feature twelve charismatic and sought-after wildlife species, found in twelve spectacular parks, and best experienced in twelve different months. These feature stories represent the wonderful diversity and opportunities found throughout the entire park system. However, these accounts should be viewed not as an end, but as a springboard into the amazing ecological richness of the parks. For example, chapter 1 is titled "March—Gray Wolves of Yellowstone." The chapter tells you:

---

1   When we refer to "national park" we are also including national monuments, recreational areas, seashores, lakeshores, historic sites, national scenic rivers, and other designations—all managed by the National Park Service.

- why Yellowstone National Park is the best place to see wolves,
- why March is the best time to view wolves in the park,
- where in the park your chances are best for seeing wolves,
- where to get current information regarding the wolves in the park,
- how wolves influence the ecosystem,
- about the conservation story of wolves,
- about other animals to look for in wolf habitat, and
- what other parks have wolf-viewing opportunities.

Perhaps even more importantly than being a guide to viewing wildlife in parks, this book is a celebration. It's a celebration of our precious wildlife heritage. And it's a celebration of these public lands that belong to all Americans. These animals and these parks are America. It's impossible to fathom America without these animals and without the parks in which they reside. Even urban city dwellers find satisfaction just knowing that there are wolves in Yellowstone or alligators in the Everglades. These places and these animals are a part of our legacy, part of our shared story, and part of what makes us a country.

Hopefully, this book will inspire Americans to get out and experience wild America. We expect that many people who buy this book are predisposed to get outdoors and view wildlife. However, many other people are not so inclined. We hope this book sparks an interest for the latter group. We lament the apparent decrease in outdoor activities by the American public, a trend that is bad both for our collective well-being and for our priceless natural resources—natural resources that require an involved, knowledgeable, and caring public. A trek into a national park is not only good for the body, it is mental exercise as well. Perhaps nowhere is that exercise needed as much as it is with our children. Fortunately, children are innately eager to explore and discover. To them a hiking trail through the forest of a small park is an adventure on par with what Lewis and Clark experienced. So we encourage people to get the kids off the couch and take them on a wildlife "safari" in a national park. Yes, one can be found just a few miles down the road. Neither you nor they will soon forget it.

Wildlife Watching in America's National Parks

⟆ Introduction

Wildlife in National Parks

*The further we become separated from
that pristine wilderness and beauty,
the more pleasure does the mind
of enlightened man feel
in recurring those senses.*
George Catlin—*North American Indians* (1832)

George Catlin and other nineteenth-century painters, photographers, and authors helped popularize America's western frontier. To urban Easterners, the images and stories from these frontier artists inspired romantic visions of majestic mountains, vast prairies, and pristine streams, at a time when much of the wildness of the eastern United States was being lost. The Yellowstone region, in what would eventually become northwest Wyoming, was especially magical to eastern audiences due in part to Thomas Moran's watercolors and William Henry Jackson's photographs. These beautiful paintings and images spurred public support to protect these unspoiled lands. The most obvious solution, although unprecedented, was to simply set the land aside in protected federal ownership. In 1872 Congress established the Yellowstone area as America's first national park, to be set aside and protected for the "enjoyment and wonderment of people." Yellowstone National Park immediately began attracting tourists who marveled at the hot springs, geysers, waterfalls, and other physical wonders. Eventually, Yellowstone would become the most well-known national park in the world—a cherished natural treasure. But perhaps the real legacy of Yellowstone is the precedent it established. It laid the groundwork for creating other parks and protected areas in what would eventually become the National Park System.

Although Yellowstone National Park was created primarily to protect the scenic and geologic wonders, it soon became apparent that the park was vital to protecting some of America's vanishing wildlife species. Unregulated hunting throughout the country, in some cases bordering on slaughter, had decimated many wildlife populations. Some species, such as the passenger pigeon and Carolina parakeet, would never recover. And habitat destruction was threatening other species, including many that were not hunted. By late in the nineteenth century the American bison—an iconic species once found in unfathomable numbers—was essentially gone in the wild. Yet there was still a small herd in the remote interior of Yellowstone National Park. Park rangers soon recognized the importance and urgency of protecting that small, priceless herd. They invested considerable time and effort, and even risked their lives, to prevent poaching of the bison and other game species in the park.

Whereas the nineteenth century was marked by wildlife slaughter and habitat destruction, the beginning of the twentieth century marked the birth of the conservation movement, a movement that coincided with the election of President Theodore Roosevelt. His experience living in an isolated cabin in the rugged badlands of North Dakota—a region that would eventually become the site of a national park that bears his name—instilled in him a passionate concern for wildlife, an understanding of the issues, and a conservation ethic. He witnessed firsthand the disappearing wildlife populations and the loss of wild places. And he knew intrinsically that outdoor activities were good for the mind and body. He took those observations and experiences with him to Washington, where he used his bully pulpit to lead and inspire congressional action to expand the number of forest reserves, wildlife preserves (refuges), and national parks. And when Congress failed to act fast enough to set aside such areas, he charged ahead with establishing and protecting public lands using other means, such as the authority granted him under the Antiquities Act of 1906 (which gave the executive branch the authority to establish national monuments). Eventually, the National Park System would be comprised of hundreds of national park units scattered throughout the country. The sites would protect forests, mountains, seashores, oceans, rivers, prairies, wetlands, homesteads, forts, and other scenic and historic features—and the wildlife found therein.

History of Wildlife Conservation in Parks

For most of us, knowledge of our world comes largely through sight, yet we look about with such unseeing eyes that we are partially blind.
Rachel Carson—*The Sense of Wonder* (1965)

Many of the early visitors to Yellowstone National Park viewed the geology and scenery with a sense of wonder and awe, feeling satisfied in their experience and their visit. But to many others, something was missing—it was the large herds of bison and other game animals. To rectify this, park management took some much-needed actions, such as stopping poaching. In some cases park rangers even put their lives on the line to protect these species. However, some of the park's other early management actions are now viewed as misguided and inappropriate. For example, early wildlife management projects at Yellowstone included "ranch-like" management of bison, elk, and deer with the "wild" animals being fenced in and put on display for park visitors. At the same time, large predators such as wolves, coyotes, and mountain lions were deemed a threat to the desirable game animals and were killed indiscriminately. The predator control soon expanded to include smaller predators such as bobcats, foxes, river otters, and even pelicans. Although there were objections by a few park biologists (and at that time, there were only a "few" park biologists)—who recognized the value of predators to the health of ecosystems—their lonely voices could not stop the slaughter; neither could they change agency policies as predator control continued into the 1930s. Regrettably, policy change was too late to save many predators from being extirpated in the parks.

Another misguided practice in early park management was bear feeding by park staff. Some parks even staged nightly bear-feeding events by heaping garbage and food up on platforms so park tourists could sit on grandstands to view the bears. Nowhere was this more blatant and institutionalized than at Yellowstone National Park where the feeding of bears

There are fewer than one thousand black-footed ferrets in the wild. The National Park Service conserves a couple of populations and is the only agency that provides and promotes ferret-viewing opportunities. (Photo by Daniel S. Licht)

had huge public support. Yet the park biologists and others could see the problems that such feedings were causing, problems that included unhealthy bears and risks to people. Closing the bear-feeding platforms was an early test of agency resolve, and fortunately the agency prevailed. Unfortunately, that good intention of closing the bear-feeding platforms led to other problems. Bears being bears, and people being people, the bears soon began begging for handouts from people along the roads, in the campgrounds, and elsewhere, and the people happily obliged. The word "bear jam" became part of our lexicon and synonymous with western parks. Although some lauded feeding the bears, the agency did not view the sight of "begging bears" as a positive visitor experience, nor was it viewed as good for the bears. So the Park Service began aggressively enforcing laws against feeding the animals, a policy that continues to this day. Bear management at Yellowstone is a microcosm of the internal struggles within the agency in the first half of the twentieth century regarding appropriate wildlife-viewing experiences, interactions, and management.

The 1960s marked a second significant change in our ecological thinking, as the United States faced new and often insidious environmental

Historic moments in wildlife conservation in national parks

1872—Congress establishes Yellowstone National Park "as a public park or pleasuring ground for the benefit and enjoyment of the people."

1916—The Organic Act establishes a national park system, the National Park Service, and a unifying mission to "conserve . . . the wild life therein."

1932—George Wright funds, conducts, and publishes the series "Fauna of the National Parks of the United States." The reports are considered the beginning of wildlife science within the agency.

1933—Aldo Leopold, the father of wildlife management, publishes *Game Management,* considered the seminal treatise on wildlife management.

1936—First formal NPS regulations state that "parks and monuments are sanctuaries for wildlife of every sort, and all hunting, or the killing, wounding, frightening, capturing . . . is prohibited" (the regulations were subsequently modified to prohibit such activities unless explicitly allowed by Congress).

1937—Adolph Murie, a Park Service biologist, publishes "Ecology of the Coyote in Yellowstone." That report, and his subsequent report, "The Wolves of Mt. McKinley," led to the end of predator eradication programs in parks.

1963—The "Leopold Report" called for an increased role of science in park management, an ecosystem approach toward wildlife management, and for parks to be managed as a "vignette of primitive America."

1969—In *New Mexico State Game Commission v. Udall,* and subsequent decisions, the courts found that the National Park Service, and not the individual states, has the authority to manage wildlife on park lands.

1986—In *National Rifle Association v. Potter,* the courts agreed with the National Park Service that hunting be allowed only in parks where specifically authorized by Congress. The decision was affirmed by subsequent case law.

1995—Wolves are reintroduced to Yellowstone National Park.

2006—The most recent version of the NPS management policies are published. They state that the agency "will try to maintain all the components and processes of naturally evolving park ecosystems, including the natural abundance, diversity, and genetic and ecological integrity of the plant and animal species native to those ecosystems."

problems such as pesticides and pollution. The threats inspired new environmental laws such as the Endangered Species Act, the Clean Water Act, and the National Environmental Policy Act (NEPA). These laws reaffirmed and strengthened wildlife management policies both inside and outside of parks.

About the same time, the "Leopold Report" (officially known as the "Wildlife Management Report in National Parks"—1963) asserted the need for the Park Service to manage for more than just the presence or absence of charismatic species; the agency should also conserve lesser-known uncharismatic species, persecuted species such as predators, natural processes such as fire, natural conditions such as old growth forests, and natural wildlife behaviors. That landmark report, written by a group of esteemed scientists not affiliated with the agency, still guides wildlife management practices today. Although the report recommends active management and intervention when necessary (e.g., removing overabundant ungulates when a site is too small for reintroducing large predators), the spirit of the report is that whenever possible, natural and wild conditions and processes should prevail. The report eloquently summarizes that goal when it says that national parks "should represent a vignette of primitive America." In other words, the National Park Service should manage for more than just "wildlife"; it should manage for "wild life" as written and directed in the 1916 organic act that established the agency.

As the National Park Service nears its one-hundredth birthday in 2016, it is a leader in wildlife conservation with its emphasis on native species, natural conditions, and natural processes. Parks continue to be some of the last best habitats for many species. Consider that there are forty-seven sites in the United States that are designated as International Biosphere Reserves; of those, the National Park Service manages thirty. Consider also that parks conserve and protect approximately 270 endangered and threatened species, or about one-fourth of all of the listed species in the United States. But perhaps the more important story is how many more species would be listed as threatened and endangered were it not for the fact that their populations are healthy and protected within national park units.

What will the future bring for wildlife conservation in national parks? We now know that many predatory species—such as wolves and alliga-

Why is the National Park Service unique?

National parks are unique among all federal and state lands in that the agency's management policies and actions emphasize natural processes, structure, and conditions (the three themes of biological diversity). The agency defines *natural* as the absence of human dominance on the landscape. As a result of this mission, in national parks you will see predators running free and without persecution, wildfires burning in natural patterns, and insect outbreaks that end only when nature says they are ready to end. Of course, there needs to be a check to these processes in the twenty-first century, even on national park units, but more than any other federal or state agency these natural processes are allowed to proceed unfettered by human intervention.

tors—are critical for ecosystem health. But we also know that many of these species need large areas in which to operate and that they are rarely tolerated on private lands surrounding national parks. So how does the agency preserve ecosystem health in small and midsize parks when key species are missing? How or even should the agency mimic these missing predators (e.g., should the agency allow hunting to control deer and elk populations?). Similarly, what should the agency do when actions outside the park impact migration routes and movement corridors? Should the agency artificially create habitat inside the park when the animals can no longer reach or use their normal range outside the park? Climate change is another huge future concern for the agency. It seems inevitable that our climate will change, moving biomes northward or upward in elevation, but park boundaries won't move. How do we conserve species that have evolved at a certain site and in a certain climate?

National parks, despite some bumps in the road and the occasional wrong turn, have been critical to conserving our nation's wildlife resources and a model of modern wildlife conservation. Starting with the establishment of Yellowstone National Park in 1872, national parks have

Reintroducing swift fox at Badlands National Park. National parks attempt to conserve all native species. (Photo by Daniel S. Licht)

protected essential habitats for America's native wildlife. Many of the featured wildlife species in this book have climbed back from the brink of extinction thanks to national park units, and they can again be viewed in the wild. In the end that is one of the greatest accomplishments of national parks—that people can view their wildlife heritage. There is no place better to do that than in a national park.

Watching Wildlife in Parks

The enjoyment of wildlife is in proportion to its naturalness.
Aldo Leopold—*A Land Ethic* (1949)

Wildlife viewing connects us to nature. And there is no better place to watch wildlife than in a national park. The parks are open to all, the animals are relatively tolerant of people, and the habitats are natural, with only a few man-made features, if any. Furthermore, the wildlife watcher generally doesn't have to worry about conflicting uses such as hunting seasons. And in parks you can best witness the full diversity of wildlife that roamed America's frontier, including iconic species like bison, bears, and wolves. All this against a gallery of breathtaking scenery makes wildlife viewing in national parks an unparalleled experience.

There is no good system-wide estimate of the number of people who visit national parks primarily to view wildlife, but we can infer from individual park data that the number is enormous. Consider that 88 percent of the visitors to Grand Teton National Park, 76 percent of the visitors to Voyageurs National Park, and 71 percent of the visitors to Everglades National Park were there to view wildlife (data from the University of Idaho Visitor Services Project). Wildlife viewing consistently ranks near the top of visitor activity surveys, especially at our large iconic parks (table 1). Then consider that in 2009 the entire National Park System received 285 million visits, accounting for 1.2 billion visitor hours! Although some of those visits were to units with little or no wildlife (e.g., the National Mall in downtown Washington, DC), many visits were to park units with abundant and charismatic wildlife. It seems irrefutable that wildlife viewing is one of the most popular activities at most parks and the primary reason for many park visits.

Part of what makes viewing wildlife in national parks so fascinating is that the visitor will never see everything. Consider that there are at least 4,847 vertebrate species (or subspecies) in national park units, and 3,988 in units in the contiguous forty-eight states (table 2). Yet that is just the tip of the iceberg as there are certainly many more vertebrate species yet to be documented (one might think that park managers know all the species in their park, but unfortunately, that is not always the case). Then

Table 1. Percentage of visitors viewing wildlife and participating in other activities at select parks

Park	Season/Year	Top Activity	Second	Third
Channel Islands	Summer 1993	Marine Watching 45%	Bird Watching 34%	Photography 33%
Denali	Summer 2006	View Scenery 93%	View Wildlife 91%	Experiencing Wilderness 57%
Everglades	Winter 2008	Nature View / Bird Watching 75%	Walking / Hiking 74%	Photography / Painting / Drawing 28%
Glacier	Summer 1990	Sightseeing 97%	Photography 89%	View Wildlife 87%
Grand Teton	Summer 2008	View Scenery / Scenic Drive 77%	Walking / Hiking 52%	View Wildlife / Nature Study / Bird Watching 42%
Great Smoky Mountains	Summer 2008	View Scenery 95%	View Wildlife 69%	Walking / Hiking 62%
Redwood	Summer 1993	Sightseeing 91%	Walking / Hiking 64%	View Wildlife / Bird Watching 39%
Rocky Mountain	Summer 2010	View Scenery 93%	Driving Trail Ridge Road 75%	View Wildlife / Bird Watching 73%
Voyageurs	Summer 1997	Sightseeing 79%	View Wildlife 76%	Fish without Guide 66%
Yellowstone	Summer 1989	View Wildlife 93%	View Thermal Features 85%	Photography 83%

Data from University of Idaho Visitor Services Project.

consider the invertebrates; the 10,000 or so of those that have been documented in park units are almost certainly a miniscule percent of the total number of species out there. Add to that the vascular and nonvascular plants, the fungi, protozoa, Monera, Chromista, and other life forms and it's obvious that the National Park System is a treasure of biological diversity. We may never know how many species there actually are within the system, but consider that Great Smoky Mountains National Park has for years been conducting an all-taxa inventory, and over 17,300 species have been documented to date in that one park, including over 900 species new to science. Estimates are that the actual number of species in that park alone may exceed 100,000.

With so many wildlife species, and with so many mysteries regarding their ecologies, the parks truly are a window to discovery, even in that small park just down the road. Furthermore, no two days exploring a

Table 2. Facts about wildlife viewing in national parks

	All Parks	Contiguous 48 States
Number of national park units	394	367
Number of park units with significant natural resources	270	243
Number of documented or expected species[1]:		
Mammals	479	461
Birds	1,007	918
Reptiles	344	315
Amphibians	222	216
Fish	2,795	2,078
Vascular plants	17,657	15,803
Invertebrates	12,789	8,608

[1] Data from National Park Service database NPSpecies.

park will ever be the same. That's part of what makes wildlife watching in national parks so interesting, so challenging, and a pursuit that can last a lifetime. Visitors never know what will cross their path.

Why View Wildlife?

In wildness is the preservation of the world.
Henry David Thoreau—*Atlantic Monthly* (1862)

We would be remiss if we did not briefly mention why we think people should get outdoors and watch wildlife in its natural habitat, as this entire book is premised on the belief that such activity is beneficial and worthwhile. While there are numerous reasons that wildlife viewing is a productive undertaking, three primary reasons are that: 1) wildlife viewing is a healthy endeavor, both intellectually and physically; 2) wildlife viewing leads to understanding and appreciation, which in turn leads to support and conservation of wildlife; and 3) wildlife viewing is exciting and fun.

Numerous studies have confirmed the benefits, both mentally and physically, of frequent interactions with natural environments. Meanwhile, it is well known that some members of our population are not as physically fit as they should be. Nor is our population as knowledgeable as they should be, especially in regard to the natural environment. Today, both children and adults are engulfed by gadgets and irrelevant streams of information (at least in our opinion). Furthermore, we've lost the scientific inquisitiveness and curiosity that is critical for any civil society to progress. We believe that spending time in the outdoors watching wildlife can be an antidote to some of these ills. And we believe that our national parks are part of the prescription for restoring our collective health and well-being. Time outdoors can also strengthen the fabric of families, a growing concern in our hectic lives.

Many people enjoy viewing wildlife through nature documentaries on television; we acknowledge that such vicarious activities can be informative and entertaining, and may even inculcate a curiosity in nature, but they are no substitute for the real thing. An authentic wildlife-viewing experience, against the backdrop of nature's majesty, stirs both the body

12   Introduction

Why national parks are the best places to view wildlife

1.   The National Park Service's mission mandates that the agency conserve wildlife and provide for the public's enjoyment of such wildlife.

2.   Most park units do not allow hunting so the animals are more tolerant of people. The animals are also protected from all forms of collecting, harassment, and disturbance.

3.   Parks generally contain more species than nonpark lands. Some species such as wolves, prairie dogs, and grizzly bears are not tolerated on private lands and even on some other public lands, but in national park units they are protected and conserved.

4.   Park units promote natural processes such as fire, so not only will you see wildlife, you will see the animals responding to natural processes.

5.   Parks support natural conditions. That means the wildlife will include not only young animals but also the prime age bull elk, buck deer, and other "trophy" animals that are rare on nonpark lands due to hunting.

6.   Parks have minimal anthropogenic impacts. Other than cultural resources, infrastructure, and other visitors, you will not see or hear many man-made items in national park units.

7.   Park staff is available to assist visitors in seeing wildlife and to help interpret and educate people about wildlife, and park visitor centers are usually open seven days a week and year-round.

8.   Parks have additional information such as species lists, web pages, and books (some of which are specific to the park) to help visitors see wildlife.

9.   Park units can be found in all types of habitats and ecosystems, near many urban areas, and throughout the country.

10. Parks are free or inexpensive. As more and more private lands are closed to access, or charge a fee, parks continue to be one of the more affordable and accessible lands for viewing wildlife.

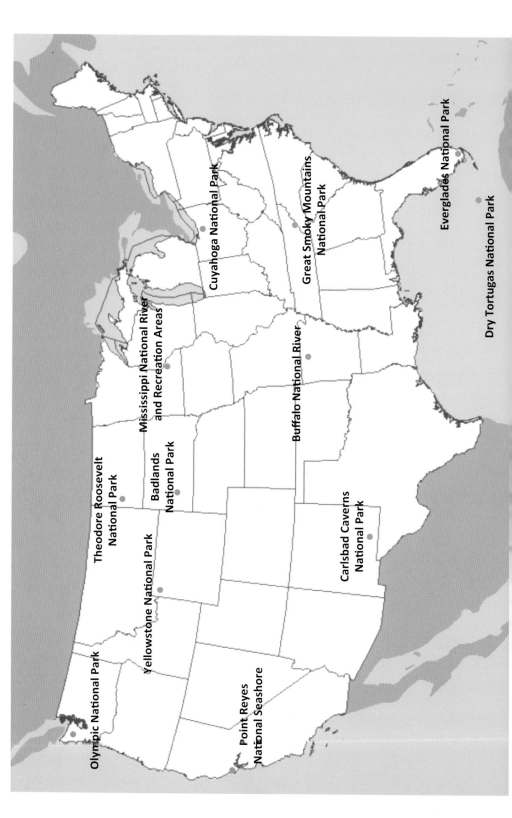

and mind in ways that television watching will never do. A real outdoor experience is unedited and unscripted. And a real outdoor experience satisfies all five senses in a way that no technology can. Lastly, a genuine outdoor experience may even trigger emotions we thought we never had (humility, awe, fear?).

Not surprisingly, we are passionate about the outdoors and we care about our natural resources. We believe the single most important thing that can be done to conserve our wildlife resources is for people to interact with wildlife. With familiarity comes appreciation, and with appreciation comes concern, and with concern comes action and support. Public enjoyment of nature and wildlife fosters a concern for both wildlife and our national parks. The historian and author Richard Sellars concluded that "the national park idea survived and ultimately flourished because it was fundamentally utilitarian." In other words, the national parks exist because people use them to recreate, to learn, and to view wildlife.

So the future of natural resource conservation depends in large part on connecting people with nature. There is no better example than that of Theodore Roosevelt. He stated many times that it was his years in the rugged Badlands of North Dakota, living in a remote cabin in the wilderness, that gave him the character to become president. It was also those years that instilled in him his conservation ethic. Although few if any of us will come close to his experiences, or reach his powerful position, we can in our own small way work to conserve wildlife, both in faraway places and in our own backyard.

The final reason we offer for people to go wildlife viewing is that we believe wildlife viewing is fun, interesting, and exciting. We will not expound on that here as we think this book, and the millions of people who already participate in wildlife viewing, are testament enough to that statement. When done right, there is no better activity.

A migrating sandhill crane. Spring is an excellent time to view wildlife as the world seems to come alive with creatures great and small. (Photo by Gordon Dietzman)

Throughout the land there may be no better season to view wildlife than spring. In much of the country the long winter silence is now filled with the chorus of frogs, the singing of birds, and the buzzing of insects, all excitedly hoping to reproduce and continue the circle of life. Spring is the season for all the senses as our eyes, ears, and nose try to take in all the sights, sounds, and smells. As the snow and cold recede and the days get longer, amazing transformations take place in the forests, prairies, and streams. Green shoots seem to magically arise from the earth and explode into blossoms of every possible color and shape, signaling spring has arrived and new life is born. For the wildlife observer spring is the time to marvel at the wonders and miracles all around us, from the humble insects to the magnificent carnivores to the sturdy oaks.

Spring comes in various forms. In the higher elevations of Yellowstone National Park, Wyoming, spring does not come easily or quickly, as winter is stubborn. Although the calendar may say *spring,* nature still says *winter.* Even in March spring is often more of a promise than a reality. At this time of the year the wild animals in Yellowstone National Park are in a precarious life-and-death struggle to make it through the last few weeks of winter. At the center of that struggle is the wolf, reintroduced to the park in part to restore the ecosystem. The wolf pursues the old, the injured, and those weakened by the long winter, even as the first signs of spring bring hope to the desperate prey. Nowhere in the lower forty-eight states is there a better opportunity to observe the struggle between an apex predator and its formidable prey than at Yellowstone National Park.

In other places the transition from winter to spring may be less extreme, although just as colorful and full of promise. That is true in places such as in Great Smoky Mountains National Park straddling the Tennessee–North Carolina border. Flower names like "spring beauty" say

Spring—why you can't wait for another day

More so than any other season, wildlife viewing in the spring cannot be put off for another day. Spring doesn't wait for anyone, especially in the North Country. The great flocks of migrating birds, the blooming wildflowers, and the pregnant mothers-to-be all know that time is of the essence. If they're going to pass on their DNA they need to move quickly, following cycles honed by countless generations before. The knowledgeable wildlife viewer knows this as well. The household chores can wait, but spring won't. Fortunately, that is one of the advantages of wildlife viewing in national park units. The knowledgeable rangers and staff know what species are being seen and where. Give them a call before venturing out and your wildlife-viewing experience will be much more successful.

it all. As these wildflowers spring to life in the forests, meadows, and fields so do hundreds of hibernating black bears. The famished animals amble out into the meadows and openings to feed on the greening vegetation. Lean and hungry, the bears busily make up for the months of fasting. Many of the sows are especially hungry as they have young cubs in tow, frolicking and romping behind them.

Few places welcome spring as much as the northern Great Plains. In winter temperatures routinely dip well below freezing and windchills can be life threatening to man and beast. Yet come spring the temperatures climb to 70 degrees or higher. This can all happen in just a matter of weeks, sometimes even days. Almost overnight the bleak, frozen landscape transforms to a vibrant green prairie. The lifeless quiet of winter is replaced with a cacophony of animal sounds. The birds are back, the hibernating animals have emerged, and the insects are buzzing. And no place is this celebration of life as exuberant as it is in the black-tailed prairie dog town. Badlands National Park in western South Dakota contains America's largest remaining prairie wilderness and is a great place to watch the playful antics of prairie dogs as well as all the other wildlife of this once-vast ecosystem, sometimes referred to as America's Serengeti.

1 ⌐ March

Gray Wolves of Yellowstone

Even in March most of Yellowstone National Park is still covered in deep snow. Although the days are getting longer and the sun is getting higher, spring still seems to take forever to come to the land, at least for some of the park's residents. At this time of the year, perched between the seasons, life hangs in the balance for the elk, bison, pronghorn antelope, and other large ungulates. Their bodies are weakened and malnourished from the long winter. On top of that, wolves are on the prowl. But it's never easy for the wolves either as they struggle to take down larger, stronger, and faster prey. This struggle between predator and prey is one of nature's greatest spectacles. At Yellowstone National Park, in northwestern Wyoming, it is often played out right in front of the wildlife watcher.

What's Remarkable about Gray Wolves?

Scientists refer to the wolf as an animal with high "plasticity," meaning that it can adapt to a wide variety of habitats and prey. Consider that the species historically ranged from the barren tundra of the Arctic to the deep, dark, boreal forests of Canada to the wide-open grasslands of the Great Plains to the scorching deserts of Mexico. All the wolf needed to survive was prey, whether it was musk ox, moose, bison, or javelina. In other words, the wolf is not really a habitat-dependent species in the con-ventional sense (i.e., vegetation), but rather a prey-dependent species. Historically, where there was prey there was wolves.

Once persecuted almost to the point of extinction in the lower forty-eight states, wolves have made a dramatic recovery in some areas. (Photo by Daniel S. Licht)

Remarkably, the wolf's prey includes some of America's largest and most dangerous species such as bison and moose. These animals can weigh up to a ton, whereas even the largest wolves may only tip the scale at around 130 pounds. It seems like a mismatch. Yet the wolf has on its side several adaptations—fine tuned by eons of evolution—including endurance, speed, and strong jaws, but most importantly, the cooperation of the pack. It's the pack that allows wolves to take down prey like the much larger bison and moose. It's the pack that allows wolves to catch swifter prey such as deer and pronghorn antelope. And it's the pack that allows wolves to overcome the many sets of eyes in the elk herd. The pack is what separates the wolf from most of North America's other large carnivores.

Yet the wolf has one more trick up its sleeve. In addition to hunting in a pack, the wolf is also a master judge of character. The wolf's ability to identify injured, sick, old, or otherwise vulnerable prey is often the difference between success and injury. Ironically, by removing unhealthy prey the wolves are what keep the herds of bison, moose, and elk healthy. In many ways, wolves are the stewards of the ecosystems in which they occur and one of nature's most remarkable animals.

Wolf Ecology

Scientists are just now beginning to understand and appreciate the important and complex role wolves play in ecosystem health. Many biologists now consider the wolf a keystone species, that is, one that influences many other species in the ecosystem. Wolves can affect ecosystems either directly, by killing prey species and therefore keeping prey populations in check, or indirectly. Consider what science has learned from the reintroduction of wolves to Yellowstone National Park.

Prior to the reintroduction of wolves to Yellowstone National Park, the park's elk herd had for decades been overabundant, which in turn led to degradation of the park's plant communities. Plants such as aspen and willow were not reaching maturity due to the heavy and relentless elk browsing. The reintroduction of wolves in 1995 has helped reduce elk numbers to a level more in balance with the ecosystem (about 90 percent of the diet of Yellowstone wolves is elk). Elk are no longer viewed as overabundant. But there's more to the story than the numbers. Watch how the two species interact. Just the presence of wolves tends to keep the elk alert and on the move, which is good for the vegetation. Prior to the reintroduction

Gray wolf feeding on an elk kill at Yellowstone National Park. (Photo by Daniel S. Licht)

of wolves the elk would loiter in aspen groves, spending little time watching for danger, and more time constantly chewing on the buds and leaves, effectively stopping the trees' regrowth. But now with wolves nearby the elk spend much less time feeding in these areas, which in turn allows the aspen stands to grow. Scientists have coined this phenomenon the "ecology of fear."

With fewer elk, and with those remaining elk spending less time in the young hardwood stands, the groves of aspen, willow, and other trees have recovered. This has benefited songbirds and all kinds of other wildlife. Scientists often call this type of response a "trophic cascade" as a change in one species (e.g., reintroducing wolves) can result in a change in

What do wolves have to do with songbirds?

As it turns out, a lot. Ornithologists (people who study birds) have long known that aspen, cottonwood, and willow stands provide habitat for a large number of songbirds such as warblers, vireos, and tanagers. This is true at Yellowstone National Park. However, the deciduous woodland habitats at Yellowstone had been degraded due to an overabundance of elk and other browsing animals. In many places, the young trees simply could not grow out of the reach of the browsers. But the presence of wolves changed that dynamic, as the wolves quickly reduced ungulate numbers and their presence limited the amount of time the elk spent browsing the trees. So more wolves meant less elk browsing, which meant more trees, which means more songbirds. Take a look at the aspen stands at Yellowstone National Park. You will see stands comprised of very large and old trees, many in a moribund condition. Near the base of those trees you will now see many young seedlings and saplings. But notice the absence of pole-size or middle-aged trees. That's because for several decades in the late twentieth century (a time with no wolves) the young trees were not able to grow due to the constant elk browsing.

A western tanager. Wolves reduce elk numbers, which increases vegetation growth, which increases songbird abundance. (Photo by Daniel S. Licht)

another species (e.g., fewer elk) and can change other species (e.g., more aspen and willow), which can change another group of species (e.g., more songbirds). Of course this "cascade" can trickle down even further to other organisms, such as insects. The presence of wolves, or any apex predator, can dramatically affect the health of ecosystems.

Wolf Conservation

Once found throughout essentially all of North America, the wolf was almost extirpated from the contiguous forty-eight states. In fact, by the middle of the twentieth century the only remaining wolf populations in the lower forty-eight states were the small remnant populations in northern Minnesota and the population in Isle Royale National Park in Lake Superior. But once the Endangered Species Act was passed in 1973 wolf populations began expanding as wolves from Canada naturally recolonized northwestern Montana, and wolves from Minnesota recolonized Wisconsin and the Upper Peninsula of Michigan.

However, there were doubts as to how much further wolves could expand on their own, and whether they could reach the vast protected wilderness of Yellowstone National Park, so the federal government, at the urging of conservationists, began planning for a reintroduction of wolves from Canada. The reintroduction of wolves to Yellowstone National Park in 1995 is one of the most controversial and costly wildlife management actions ever taken. Yet the effort was more than just a reintroduction of an animal to its former habitat; it was also a symbolic action showing how far the country had come in its attitudes toward predators and wildlife and how important the national parks are to wildlife conservation.

Now, fifteen or so years later, that effort is by almost all measures a huge success. Wolves have now repopulated much of the park. And just as importantly, they are now fulfilling their keystone role by controlling ungulate abundance and behavior, which keeps the ecosystem healthy for all wildlife. They are also adding immeasurably to visitor experiences as more than a million people have likely seen wolves at the park. Consider that one study found that an estimated 325,000 visitors saw wolves in 2005, and that wolves increased ecotourism spending by $35 million in that same year. The restoration of the wolf to Yellowstone is arguably one of the greatest conservation stories ever told.

Parks with Gray Wolves

Yellowstone National Park, Wyoming

The world's first national park is also one of North America's premier wildlife-viewing locations. Established in 1872, the 2.2 million-acre park contains snow-capped mountains, dark forests, rolling prairies, as well as famous geysers, hot springs, and waterfalls. The park also hosts one of the most natural and complete wildlife communities of any site in the contiguous forty-eight states. In fact, every species that was present when explorers first arrived may still be there today.

For most of the year Yellowstone National Park is wide open to visitors with countless places to go and scenic wonders to explore. But in March many of these places are still closed and inaccessible. In fact, the only road open to wheeled vehicles is the highway from Mammoth (and Gardiner) to Cooke City, Montana. Fortunately, that road goes through

Yellowstone's Lamar Valley. One of the best places in the world to view wild wolves. (Photo by Daniel S. Licht)

the Lamar Valley where some of the best wildlife viewing is. Another option for seeing the park is to take a snow coach to the Yellowstone Lodge (Old Faithful). Once there, a person can cross-country ski the groomed trails or they can head off on their own with snowshoes. Of course, safety should be paramount for any outdoor activities in Yellowstone in March; visitors should check weather forecasts and consult with park rangers prior to an outing. Although wolves are scarce around Old Faithful, there are still bison, elk, and other animals to observe. Witnessing these animals struggling to survive a Yellowstone winter gives real meaning to "survival of the fittest."

Seeing a wolf, or any predator for that matter, is a special experience, since predators are often extremely difficult to spot in the wild. This is especially true in places where predators are hunted, trapped, or otherwise persecuted. Fortunately, a visitor to Yellowstone National Park has a relatively high likelihood of seeing wolves in their natural habitat. There are several reasons for this. One, Yellowstone's wolves are protected from hunting so they don't quickly flee or hide from people. Two, Yellowstone consists of a mixture of dense forests and wide-open prairies, meadows, and floodplains; the open areas are conducive to wolf observations. Three, the prey density at Yellowstone is relatively high, which leads to relatively high wolf densities. Last, Yellowstone is the home of the "wolf watchers," a reference to the people who passionately follow and watch the park's wolves. These "wolf watchers" are always happy to share tips and recent sightings with a visitor (see below for more information on the "wolf watchers").

By the end of 2009, there were at least ninety-six wolves in Yellowstone National Park, distributed among about fourteen packs and smaller groups and loners. The packs are primarily concentrated in the central and northern portions of the park. However, the location and composition of the packs can change dramatically from year to year, so where they are common one year they may be almost absent the next. This dynamic nature is due in part to strife and fights between packs as one pack may invade another pack's territory. This is all part of natural wolf behavior and dynamics. Because of the ever-changing nature of the packs we advise readers to go to the park's website or talk to a ranger for the most up-to-date information on the pack locations and composition.

Although pack members and names may change from year to year, one constant (so far) is that some of the best places to see wolves are on the stretch of road between Tower–Roosevelt Junction and the Soda Butte Creek area. Packs in this area originally went by the names of Druid and Slough Creek, but there was a dramatic reorganization in 2008. Although the pack names have changed, there are still a lot of easily viewable wolves in the area. Within this stretch of road the single best place to see wolves may be from the dirt road that heads to the Slough Creek Campground. From the road a wolf den can be viewed on the far hillside across the creek, that is, to the northwest. You will often see groups of people stationed on a small hilltop about 50 yards from the road, all armed with spotting scopes pointed toward the den area (the den is literally a mile or more away so a good scope is essential). In addition to that generally reliable site, wolves can show up almost anywhere. If they've made a kill they will hang around the site for a day or two, so wait patiently (in addition to wolves you will almost certainly see bears, coyotes, eagles, and other

2011 Yellowstone Wolf Pack Territories

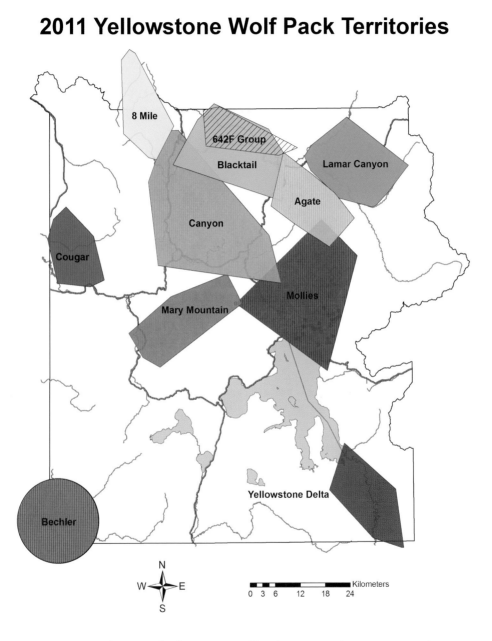

Approximate location of Yellowstone's wolf pack territories. (Courtesy National Park Service)

wildlife taking advantage of the wolf kill). As with most wildlife, morning and dusk are the best time to see or hear the wolves; however, depending in part on their hunting success they may be active any time of the day.

The interesting thing about Yellowstone and its wolves is that the visitors, more specifically the "wolf watchers," know as much about the wolves as many of the park employees. "Wolf watchers" are a small group of people who spend their time looking for and watching the park's wolves. Many are retired people who live in local communities. Some know all of the wolves by name. During the peak summer tourist season the wolf watchers can get lost in the crowds, but in March if you see any people along the Lamar Valley Road with binoculars or spotting scopes they are likely "wolf watchers." Many of them are more than happy to share with a visitor the wolves they're watching or the best places to see them. (They actually help the park with wolf monitoring by providing park employees with recent sightings, observations of kill events, and other information.)

Of course, the park visitor center in Mammoth Hot Springs is also a good place to learn about wolves and where they are being observed. There are also several books on wolves, including books specific to the Yellowstone reintroduction. As in all national parks, rangers can also provide recent sightings, information, and tips. The park's website is a great source of information as is the website of the Greater Yellowstone Science Learning Center.

MORE WILDLIFE IN WOLF TERRITORIES

Wildlife viewing doesn't get any better than in Yellowstone National Park. Large animals can be found everywhere, but of course, some places are better than others. The Lamar Valley area is great for bison, elk, and pronghorn antelope. Watch the behavior of these species; if they're intently staring in one direction or running, it's likely that a wolf or other predator is nearby. Elk, mule deer, and bighorn sheep are all common along the Gardiner Canyon Road that enters the park near Mammoth Hot Springs.

Yellowstone National Park may be the best place in North America to view a variety of large mammals, including carnivores, in their natural habitat. Here are ten large mammals that you may see during a March visit (table 3), starting with the easiest to see to the most difficult:

Table 3. Ten large mammals to see in Yellowstone wolf country

Bison	Although some bison leave the park in winter, many of these hardy animals remain to tough it out.
Elk	If the snows are still deep in March some elk may be at lower elevations outside the park, but a viewer should still see some.
Pronghorn	Deep and/or crusty snow are about the only thing that slows down a pronghorn, so look for them in areas with little snow.
Mule Deer	Mule deer are less migratory and nomadic than the other ungulates. They can be found anywhere in the park.
Coyote	March is the coyote breeding season. In addition to seeing some one should hear them as well.
Bighorn Sheep	One sometimes sees these animals licking a road surface, probably in an effort to consume road salt.
Wolf	Yellowstone's top predator. Keep an eye out for congregating ravens, magpies, and eagles as they may signal a wolf kill.
Grizzly and Black Bears	There are about 500 grizzly bears in the park. They and black bears usually emerge from hibernation around March–April
Moose	Moose numbers have remained low (about 500) at Yellowstone for the past decade, perhaps as a result of changing habitat.
Lynx	Get photos if possible as lynx and bobcats are similar. If you think you've seen a lynx contact a park ranger as soon as possible.

Yellowstone "wolf watchers." In March many of the people at the park are wolf watchers. (Photo by Gary W. Vequist)

March–Gray Wolves of Yellowstone   31

Wolves (right) are larger and stockier than coyotes (left). Coyotes usually run from wolves, but this one is probably defending its den site. (Photo by Daniel S. Licht)

Coyotes warrant additional discussion because of their fascinating history at the park and their ecological relationship to wolves. Prior to the reintroduction of wolves in 1995 the coyote was the "top dog" at the park and had been for many decades. When wolves were reintroduced the coyote's world changed almost overnight. Wolves view the smaller coyotes as competitors and will, at times, kill them. Not surprisingly, soon after the reintroduction of wolves to the park the coyote abundance in Yellowstone decreased and the coyotes began traveling in smaller packs, probably in an effort to be less conspicuous to the larger wolves. It appears that the two species have now reached an equilibrium, with both existing in healthy populations. In fact, coyotes sometimes benefit from wolves as they can often sneak a meal from wolf-killed carrion.

Another noteworthy Yellowstone species that has a complex relationship with wolves is the grizzly bear. Some Yellowstone grizzly bears are just starting to emerge from hibernation in March. These bears are hungry and looking for food. At this time of the year the best source of food is wolf-killed carrion. Of course, if the wolves are present at the kill the bear may have to fight for its meal. The outcome is usually determined by the size of the bear and the number of wolves at the kill (a large bear can usually fend off three or fewer wolves, but it depends on a lot of factors, including which animal is the hungriest). Look for grizzly bears in the Lamar Valley as well as around the Tower–Roosevelt Junction area. A good wildlife watcher knows to keep an eye on the other wildlife species such as ravens, magpies, and eagles as they often congregate near a wolf kill, and if they are present, wolves and bears may be in the vicinity. Of course, one should not approach such kills. Remember, Yellowstone's cardinal rule is "do not approach wildlife." In fact, you will generally find that you can best view wildlife from the roads as the animals tend to be nonchalant about people and cars on roads, but they get nervous when they see people away from the roads.

Other Parks with Wolves

The future looks promising for the gray wolf, especially within national parks. Twenty-seven units report the presence of wolves, although only eleven are from the contiguous forty-eight states. Some of those units are tiny historic parks that a wolf occasionally passes through (e.g., Grand Portage National Monument in Minnesota). It's likely that over time more parks will report the presence of wolves, albeit the occurrences will mostly consist of transient animals or very small populations, as most park units are too small to support multiple packs of wolves. The following parks support wolves:

Grand Teton National Park, Wyoming
This 96,000-acre park lies just south of Yellowstone National Park, includes similar habitat, and is considered part of the Greater Yellowstone Ecosystem. There are no barriers to wolf movement between the two parks so it is not surprising that wolves from Yellowstone recolonized Grand Teton. There are about five packs of wolves that call the park home, with the Huckleberry pack being almost entirely within the safety of the park boundaries. Much of the territories of the other four packs lie

These three wolves are all from the same pack. At Yellowstone one will find black, gray, and blond color phases. (Photo by Daniel S. Licht)

outside of the park boundary, meaning the animals are at risk of being shot. This also means the packs will generally be a lot less stable in terms of composition, behavior, and social interactions. For the wildlife observer it means that seeing these wolves is comparatively less likely as they may become more nocturnal, stay closer to cover, and have a greater flight distance from humans. On the plus side, Grand Teton National Park is a great park for seeing moose, elk, bison, and other wildlife that are prey for wolves.

North Cascades National Park and Ross Lake National Recreation Area
In contrast with the reintroduced population in Yellowstone National Park (which subsequently expanded to Grand Teton National Park), wolves from Canada naturally recolonized North Cascades National Park and the neighboring Ross Lake National Recreation Area. The first wolf was documented in 1984, and reproduction apparently first occurred around 1990. The parks contain some very rugged mountainous country so getting a good population estimate is difficult, but it's believed that

there is only a pack or two present. Seeing wolves at the park is also very difficult due to that same rugged terrain, the dense forests, and the absence of roads, so one may have to settle for seeing their sign or hearing them. Even if one does not see a wolf one still has a quality outdoor experience just knowing they are in wolf country. The two parks are one of the few places in the lower forty-eight states that still support two other endangered wilderness carnivores, the wolverine and the lynx.

Voyageurs National Park, Minnesota

Wolves in Minnesota?—you betcha! There are more wolves in Minnesota (about 3,000 as of 2010) than in the other forty-eight contiguous states combined. Voyageurs National Park, located in extreme northern Minnesota along the border with Canada, is prime north woods wolf habitat. The park probably supports about thirty wolves; however, seeing wolves here is not easy as the park is comprised of a patchwork of dense forests and lakes. In fact, the best way for summer visitors to get to the

Wolf watching is an auditory as well as a visual experience. (Photo by Daniel S. Licht)

backcountry and numerous campgrounds is by boat. In March about the only way to get around is via cross-country skis or snowshoes (snowmobiles are allowed in some areas). The odds of seeing wolves are better in March as the animals may be observed crossing the numerous ice-covered lakes. Voyageurs National Park is about a two-hour drive from Ely, Minnesota, the home of the International Wolf Center. The center has a large visitor center, interpretive displays, and a small population of captive wolves. The center also offers several outdoor programs and trips for wolf watchers.

Isle Royale National Park, Michigan

It is not possible to discuss wolves and national parks without mentioning Isle Royale National Park. This island park in western Lake Superior, located about 13 miles from the Minnesota coastline, has a fascinating story to tell. Prior to European settlement the island and nearby mainland were inhabited by caribou and, one assumes, the occasional wolf pack. However, hunting eliminated the caribou and wolves. At the same time, logging of the old growth forests made the habitat less conducive to the woodland caribou but created ideal conditions for moose. It is often reported that the first moose swam to the island around 1909. With no predators on the island their population soon exploded and began destroying the park's vegetation. Then around 1949 a single pair of wolves (a conclusion based on genetic analysis of the wolves currently on the island) found their way across the frozen surface of Lake Superior and colonized the island. Over time the wolf population grew to two to three packs. In the past several decades the twenty or so wolves and the five hundred or so moose have coexisted in a dynamic predator-prey relationship with populations of both species waxing and waning. For most of that period scientists have been monitoring the two populations. The park is now world famous for this unique outdoor research laboratory, so much so that the site is designated an International Biosphere Reserve.

Although famous for wolf ecology and research, the island is not well known for wolf watching. This is due in part to the dense forests, but also due in part to the fact that the island is only accessible to the public from May to October (it is the only major national park to close entirely for a season and the least visited national park in the lower forty-eight states).

Isle Royale National Park in Lake Superior is world famous for its long-term study of wolves and moose. National parks not only conserve wildlife, they are also fascinating and priceless laboratories for understanding our environment. (Photo by Daniel S. Licht)

During the summer tourist season commercial tour boats depart from Grand Portage, Minnesota, and Houghton and Copper Harbor, Michigan. Visitors may also reach the island via private boat or floatplane. Keep in mind that dogs are not allowed on the island for fear they may transmit disease to the resident wolf population. Although the island's wolves are seldom seen, their tracks and scat might be observed almost anywhere, and their howls can occasionally be heard. Many species found on the mainland, such as black bears, white-tailed deer, and coyotes, are not found on the island. Although that may be a negative for the wildlife watcher, it does help scientists better understand the complex wolf-moose predator-prey relationship without the confounding factors of other species. That is yet another value of the National Park System: the units are areas in which to conduct research to help us better understand the complex world in which we live and our impact on it.

2 ⚜ April

Black Bears of the Great Smoky Mountains

Black bears are generally a difficult animal to see. In most of North America they prefer the deep, dark forests and tend to be more active at night. In places where they are hunted they can become even more reclusive. Yet in Great Smoky Mountains National Park in April the bears are relatively easy to see as they venture out into the greening meadows to feed on the nutritious spring vegetation. The sows are often accompanied by their newborn cubs that—to the delight of the wildlife observer—are usually more interested in playing than in feeding. Combine that with some spectacular scenery, and the sights, sounds, and smells of spring, and the visitor has a fantastic wildlife-viewing opportunity.

What's Remarkable about Black Bears?

Black bears are remarkable animals for a variety of reasons, including their ability to hibernate, their voracious appetite, and their powerful bond between mother and cubs. But perhaps the most remarkable feature of black bears is their incredible sense of smell. It's often stated that bears may have the best sense of smell of any animal on earth, probably several times better than a bloodhound's and perhaps 100,000 times better than a human's. Several anatomical features give bears this amazing ability, including: the surface area inside a bear's nine-inch nostrils is enormous, providing for more olfactory receptors; the nostrils contain hundreds of tiny muscles the bear uses to manipulate the nose for optimal smelling;

Black bears generally stay in the forest. (Photo by Sam Hobbs)

bears have a special organ in the roof of the mouth that enhances their sense of smell; and the portion of the bear's brain that responds to signals from the nose is extremely well developed. This sense of smell is legendary. Consider the adage attributed to American Indians: "a feather fell in the forest; the eagle saw it, the deer heard it, and the bear smelled it."

So prominent is this sense of smell in a bear's day-to-day activities that it's as if the nose is the bear, and the rest of the animal is along for the ride (you've heard the saying about the "tail wagging the dog"—with bears it seems that the "nose wags the bear"). It's believed that a bear can detect the scent of food from miles away. That olfactory ability is especially important in early spring as food is still in short supply. If the bear is a sow with newborn cubs it's even more important that she find food. The cubs in tow may seem more concerned with playing and exploring, yet their nose and brain are taking it all in and storing it in memory banks for when they need to fend for themselves; the cubs' success in life will only go as far as their nose will take them.

The Bear's Diet

Black bears are "omnivores," meaning they will eat almost any edible thing they find; however, in the wild a black bear's diet is about 85 percent vegetable matter. Yet that percentage can vary greatly from place to place and season to season. For example, in places where wolves are present black bears may have more of a meat diet in the form of wolf-killed carrion. Such carrion can be especially important in early spring before "green up." Once the grasses and forbs emerge the bears readily turn to the nutritious vegetation.

In summer the bear's diet may switch to blueberries, blackberries, huckleberries, and other fruits. At Great Smoky Mountains National Park in summer the bears are often found near cherry trees. Grubs, which the bear finds by tearing apart decaying logs, also supplement a black bear's summer diet. On occasion a black bear will manage to capture a newborn deer fawn or elk calf. In fall the bear's diet switches to acorns, hickory nuts, and other protein-rich mast, which are perfect for building fat reserves for hibernation. In preparation for the long winter slumber a bear may consume up to 20,000 calories a day. By the time they enter the den they may have doubled their weight from the preceding spring.

As winter approaches the bears begin looking for a den. They often den under large deadfalls. Bears at Great Smoky Mountains National Park in Tennessee and North Carolina are somewhat unusual in that they occasionally den high above the ground in standing hollow trees (a denning resource that may be more available in the park because much of the area has been protected from logging the old trees). Despite what Hollywood and the authors of children's books say, they hardly ever den in a cave. By the time they emerge from their den in the spring they may have lost 40 percent of their pre-denning weight.

Bear Conservation

Although once greatly reduced in abundance and distribution due to hunting, the adaptable black bear has made a remarkable comeback in

Although black bear attacks on humans are extremely rare, it is best to use caution and good judgment. (Courtesy National Park Service)

the eastern United States. By some estimates there are now in excess of 600,000 black bears in North America. In fact, in some areas they have recovered to the point that some view them as a nuisance or pest species. With so many bears roving North America you would think they are easy to see; however, they're often most active at night, and where they are hunted they can become very reclusive. That's why national parks are one of the best places to see a black bear.

For decades the sight of roadside "panhandler bears" at Yosemite, Yellowstone, and Great Smoky Mountains National Parks defined black bears and symbolized national parks for much of the public. The site of bears begging for food reinforced the image of bears as cuddly and affable (like a teddy bear) and the image of a long line of cars in a "bear jam" epitomized the national park experience. Yet for the safety of both the bears and park visitors the feeding of bears (and all wildlife) is now prohibited in all national parks. That may dismay some, but today a visitor who sees a bear in a national park is watching a truly wild animal capable of surviving on its own wits and skills; in fact, studies have shown that these truly wild bears can live twice as long as "panhandler" bears.

Do bears hibernate?

It depends on your definition. True hibernation is a deep and long slumber accompanied by a dramatic drop in body temperature and bodily functions. True hibernators wake slowly. However, some animals go into a "torpor" that can be similar to hibernation, but is often of shorter duration with a more modest drop in body temperature. The animals wake quickly. Some scientists place bears in the latter category as they only have a modest drop in body temperature and they sometimes wake to move around. Consider that some small hibernators have metabolic rates only 2 percent of their normal rates, whereas a black bear's metabolism is about 25 percent of its summer rates. Yet other scientists feel that such a drop in bodily functions warrants the title of hibernator. Regardless of what you call it, it's an amazing adaptive strategy that allows bears to survive in ecosystems where they would not otherwise be able to.

Parks with Black Bears

Great Smoky Mountains National Park, Tennessee–North Carolina
Entering the 520,000-acre Great Smoky Mountains National Park is like entering a time capsule. In addition to seeing some of the oldest mountains in the world (200+ million years), a visitor will see ancient forests shrouded in mists, historic farms cut out of the frontier wilderness, and much of our wildlife heritage. In fact, the park has so retained its wilderness character that it was the site of the 1950s Disney movie, *Davy Crockett, King of the Wild Frontier.* The park preserves the largest tract of eastern deciduous forest left in the United States and 95 percent of the remaining stands of southern old growth forests. It's no wonder the park is one of the few sites in the United States worthy of the designation as an International Biosphere Reserve.

Great Smoky Mountains National Park truly was established by the people for the people. The idea for the park started in the 1920s with a strong grassroots community interest. Even though it was the Great Depression, school students and concerned citizens from near and far contributed small amounts of money to acquire what would become the park. They had to move quickly before the pristine old growth forests fell to the logger's ax. Eventually, federal and state support coalesced, some large benefactors came on board, and one-half million acres of forests and streams were purchased and protected. Now, almost a century later, over nine million visitors come to the park annually.

Great Smoky Mountains National Park provides a wide variety of outdoor activities and adventure for the visitor, including hiking, biking, and camping. The Sugarlands and Cades Cove Visitor Centers provide a wealth of information on the outdoor activities at the park, as does the newly remodeled Oconaluftee Visitor Center. At the centers one can get a park map, wildlife checklists, and recent information on bear sightings.

Great Smoky Mountains has an estimated 1,500 black bears, or about two per square mile. Although that may not seem extremely dense, it is on the high end for black bears or any large carnivore. More importantly, from the perspective of the wildlife watcher, the black bears are unhunted and therefore more tolerant of being watched than bears in hunted areas.

Safety in Bear Country

Okay, we just told you that Great Smoky Mountains National Park has some of the highest bear densities in the world, and that the visitor should get out and hike, bicycle, and camp. That, of course, may raise safety concerns with some people. Truth be told, people have little to fear from black bears and should be much more worried about traffic on the roads. Having said that, we feel compelled to state the obvious and say that one should never provoke or encourage a confrontation with a bear, as that can be bad for both the visitor and the bear. So we provide the following tips and guidance.

- Watch bears from a safe distance. If there is commonsense guidance, that is it. Yet it is more than just guidance; in most parks it is also a rule and violators can be ticketed. For example, at Great Smoky Mountains National Park the rule is that one cannot willfully approach within 50 yards of a bear, or any distance that disturbs or displaces the bear.

- Do not get between bears and food (e.g., carrion) or between a sow and her young. Yes, another commonsense rule (see the pattern?). If a bear is acting agitated or disturbed, back off (even if the reason is unknown; there could be a cub or carrion nearby that one doesn't see).

- Keep the campground/picnic area clean and odor free. Once again, this is not only good guidance but also an enforceable rule in most parks. Always dispose of garbage in bear-proof containers (all park picnic areas and frontcountry campgrounds have such containers). If you must carry food, do so in odor-proof containers. When camping in the backcountry use cable systems to lift food and trash (and preferably an entire backpack) up out of the reach of bears.

- Always have an escape route planned. That way one is prepared for the unexpected. Ultimately, avoiding confrontations is best for the visitor's safety and the bear's.

April is a great time to view the bears as they have just emerged from hibernation and the crowds of people are less than they are in the summer months (the peak bear viewing may actually be in late summer, but that's also when the crowds are the largest). The fields and meadows near Cades Cove are a prime location. Early morning is best as the bears are most active and auto traffic is light. There are numerous strategically placed pull-offs along the park roads from which one can safely view the bears. Use binoculars to scan the edge of the forests for foraging bears—good optics will really help bring out black bears otherwise obscured in the shaded forests. And don't be fooled into thinking that all black bears are black; some are cinnamon or brown (although those colors are more common in western populations).

Even when bears themselves are hard to find they often deposit clues. When looking for bears search for a telltale sign of bear activity such as tracks, overturned logs, or clawed trees. One of the more noticeable signs is bear droppings—they actually do defecate (to put it delicately) in the woods. A large plate-size dropping full of seeds, vegetable matter, and perhaps some hair and bones is good evidence that one is in bear country. In more open areas one may find fields of berries and other fruiting plants that have been picked clean, trampled, and otherwise torn up. Deeper in the forest one may find dug-up plants such as skunk cabbage. A favorite food at Great Smoky Mountains National Park is the plant squawroot, also known as "bear corn." This nonphotosynthesizing plant resembles a cob of corn growing from the roots of oak trees. Breeding-age males (known as bruins) make another bear sign; they mark their large territories by using their claws to scratch long, deep, vertical grooves in "bear trees." The higher up on the tree the scratches, the bigger the bruin. For many people, simply knowing they are in bear country greatly elevates their alertness and outdoor awareness.

Spring wildlife watching is also a great time for wildflower viewing, especially flora such as this trillium. (Photo by Gary W. Vequist)

Few parks can match Great Smoky Mountains National Park's amazing biological diversity. That diversity starts with the plants. Over 1,600 flowering plants have been documented in the park. The park is especially well known for its brilliant spring wildflower displays, including such standouts as spring beauty, wild geranium, Dutchman's breeches, Jack-in-the-pulpit, trillium, and various violets. The park conducts a "Spring Wildflower Pilgrimage" that attracts people from far and wide. The park is also known to have more kinds of native trees (about one hundred) than any other park in America. This lush vegetation, combined with the high humidity and 55+ inches of rain annually (more than any other site in the contiguous forty-eight states outside of the Pacific Northwest), is what creates the namesake *blue mist* or *smoke.*

The high humidity also benefits a fascinating, but often overlooked group of wildlife: the salamanders. In fact, Great Smoky Mountains National Park bills itself as the salamander capital of the world, with at least thirty different species. At times it seems as if one can be found

Keep food out of reach of bears; it's safe for both you and the bear (Photo by Gary W. Vequist)

under every rock and log. So abundant are the salamanders that there may be more of them than all the other vertebrates combined! Of special note are the various species of lungless salamanders. As the name implies, these evolutionarily bizarre salamanders have no lungs, rather, they breathe through their skin and the linings of their mouths and throats. April is a great time to see this diversity of salamanders, or as the locals call them, "spring lizards" (true lizards are, of course, reptiles and a totally different organism, but we digress).

For another out-of-the-ordinary wildlife-watching experience visit the park a couple of months later for the evening firefly (a.k.a., lightning bug) spectacle. Come June countless swarms of fireflies gather in the forest meadows and perform their twilight mating ritual. Members of one of the species of firefly at the park actually synchronize their flashing lights so thousands of little lights blink on and off in unison. So popular is this event that the park runs buses from the Sugarlands Visitor Center to some of the best firefly-viewing sites.

If you truly want to experience the biological diversity of the park and contribute to a good cause at the same time then contact the park regarding their All Taxa Biological Inventory. This ambitious undertaking is an attempt to identify and document all the living organisms in the park (one might think that parks have already done this, but regrettably, that is not the case). So far over 17,000 species have been documented, but that is likely just the tip of the biological iceberg; the actual number may be up toward 100,000 species. No, one doesn't need to be an expert in fungi or millipedes to participate. What the park rangers need is for people to go out in the field and help with the searching and collecting. Who knows, a visitor might discover a species new to science.

When it comes to wildlife "watching" at Great Smoky Mountains National Park remember to use the ears as much as the eyes. This is especially true for bird watching. A skilled bird "watcher"—who uses both eyes and ears—can identify one hundred species a day at the park (the park has more than 240 bird species). The following ten bird species (table 4) are representative of the forest ecosystem and are worth looking and listening for:

Table 4. Ten forest birds worth pursuing at Great Smoky Mountains National Park in the spring

Carolina Chickadee	They and their cousin, the black-capped chickadee, call out their name with a "chick-a-dee" call.
Scarlet Tanager	One of the most beautiful birds in North America, and also a melodic songster.
Cerulean Warbler	A species of conservation concern because they need very large unfragmented forests for their breeding habitat.
Carolina Wren	Like all wrens, this diminutive bird has an amazingly loud call, which it seems to never tire of.
Ovenbird	Nothing says spring in the forest like the enthusiastic "teacher-teacher-teacher" call of the ovenbird.
Wood Thrush	This relatively plain-colored bird has one of the most beautiful songs of any bird.
Rose-Breasted Grosbeak	Another colorful songster, the park is at the southern edge of their breeding range.
Mockingbird	Found on the edge of forests and in urban areas, this common songster is the state bird of Tennessee.
Wild Turkey	The wild turkey can actually be found in a variety of ecosystems, but the eastern forest is a classic habitat.
Yellow-Billed Cuckoo	The name alone makes this bird worth pursuing. They are known for calling frequently before thunderstorms.

Of all of the birds calling and displaying in spring perhaps none are as entertaining as the wild turkey. Turkeys are found throughout the Great Smokies in almost every habitat, but they are most at home in the oak-hickory mixed-deciduous forests interspersed with openings. In spring the male turkeys, known as *gobblers* or *toms* (young males are known as *jakes*) venture out into the forest openings to attract females. The birds strut about with their chests pumped out, their tail feathers spread wide, and their heads turned a scarlet red or brilliant blue. And then to top off the impressive display they give the classic turkey gobble, a sound that echoes from ridgetop to ridgetop. At times several males may "strut their stuff" and gobble in unison while the females "seem" indifferent. Occasionally a brief fight may break out between two males, but the quarrel usually ends nonviolently after much grandstanding and blustering. Eventually, a female acquiesces to a particularly impressive "tom" and the cycle of life starts anew.

Spring is the mating season for wild turkeys. Early morning is the best time to hear the males gobbling in an effort to attract females. (Photo by Daniel S. Licht)

Other Parks with Bears

Black bears are now common in many national park units; in fact, 123 units now list black bears as present or probably present. We list some of the better parks for seeing black bears from various parts of the country. We also list two parks that host brown bears, the larger cousin of the black bear. Although the brown bears found in Yellowstone National Park are often referred to as grizzlies, they are now considered the same species as the salmon-eating brown bears in Alaska.

Shenandoah National Park, Virginia

Nowadays this park is densely forested and supports about five hundred black bears, but in 1935 when the park was established the site had been almost entirely logged over and black bears were extirpated. Given time and protection the forests recovered and the bears returned along with other wildlife. The park—only a short two-hour drive from our nation's capitol—is an oasis of wildlife and solitude in an increasingly urban landscape. A popular way to visit the park is to take the 105-mile Skyline Drive, a long and windy road that traces the primary ridgetop in the park (the speed limit is 35 mph, so plan accordingly). Black bears and other wildlife are commonly seen from the road. Before visiting, check the park website for road conditions as roads may be closed due to weather, prescribed fire, construction, and other reasons.

Delaware Water Gap National Scenic River, New Jersey–Pennsylvania

Delaware Water Gap is a famous notch in the Appalachian Mountains between New Jersey and Pennsylvania through which the Delaware River flows. The Gap was once considered a possible site for a dam, but fortunately, the dam was never built and the land that had been purchased for the reservoir now comprises the Delaware Water Gap National Recreation Area (one of the first victories for the fledgling environmental movement in the United States). Today, this scenic river valley provides excellent habitat for hundreds of black bears and other wildlife. Numerous trails branch off from the historic Old Mine Road (America's oldest commercial highway) into the hardwood forests. Backpackers on the Appalachian Trail and other hiking routes through the park regularly report black bear sightings.

Yosemite National Park, California

Yosemite Valley is known for its towering mountains, magnificent granite cliffs, and spectacular waterfalls. People travel to the park from throughout the world to view the scenery, but some also see bears in their natural habitat. Although the park only has three hundred to five hundred bears (or about one per every three square miles), the bears have historically been relatively easy to see. This is due primarily to the "panhandling bears." In times past many of these problem bears may have been drawn out of the high country because of visitors' food and garbage. Pickings were so good at the campgrounds that some bears stayed active all winter. Strict requirements are now in place regarding food storage, and the bears that are seen in the park are better able to fend for themselves.

Sequoia and Kings Canyon National Parks, California

Sequoia National Park is America's second oldest national park and the home of the largest living thing on earth, the giant sequoia trees (the species' scientific name is *Sequoiadendron giganteum*). Kings Canyon National Park also includes giant sequoias such as the towering General Grant tree (the world's second-largest tree and the only living object declared a "national shrine"). Black bears are considered common in both of these Sierra Nevada parks. Note that black bears in this part of the world may be brown, cinnamon, or blond (the true brown bear, a.k.a. grizzly, is extinct in California). To protect the bears and people, proper food storage is required, so plan accordingly.

Yellowstone National Park, Wyoming

The days of Yellowstone's "panhandler bears" peering into car windows for handouts are over, but you should view that as a good thing. Yellowstone's bears can again survive on their own. And even without these handouts, the bears are still very viewable. With a little bit of effort, say a day or two driving the park's roads, you should see bears foraging in their natural habitat for carrion, vegetation, fish, and other healthy food. That includes the black bear's larger cousin, the grizzly bear. But you will rarely see the two species in close proximity; black bears try to stay out of the way of the larger and more powerful grizzly. Grizzlies need large expanses of wilderness to survive, perhaps more than any other critter in North America. That's why the vast four-million-acre Greater Yellowstone Ecosystem is the last stronghold of the bear in the lower forty-eight states (even then, that immense area probably supports no more than six hundred grizzlies). Grizzly bears at Yellowstone can often be seen in the large sagebrush prairies and valleys, such as the Lamar and Hayden Valleys, feeding on roots, ground squirrels, and other items.

Telling grizzlies and black bears apart can be tricky, even for experienced wildlife watchers. Although grizzlies are almost always a grizzled

A brown bear and the bear-viewing platforms at Katmai National Park. (Photo by Daniel S. Licht)

brown color, black bears can be black, brown, blond, or other colors. Another useful characteristic is that grizzly bears tend to be larger than black bears, with adult male grizzlies averaging 500 pounds whereas adult male black bears average about half that. A good distinguishing characteristic, but one that takes a bit of a trained eye, is that grizzlies tend to have large shoulder humps. These humps are especially noticeable as the bear walks with the hump shifting from side to side. A distinguishing behavioral characteristic is that black bears regularly climb trees, whereas grizzlies do not (at least not typically; in nature there are always exceptions). Lastly, a grizzly has very large protruding claws on its large feet, whereas black bear claws tend to be smaller both in absolute terms and in terms of not protruding out the foot pad as far. Of course, we hope a reader is never close enough to a wild bear that he or she can use that identifying characteristic.

Katmai National Park, Alaska

We have generally avoided talking about Alaska parks as they are not easy or inexpensive for most Americans to get to, but we have to make an exception for Katmai National Park. This park and its brown bears are so world famous and spectacular that the park should be on every wildlife-watcher's bucket list. (Brown bears are the same species as the grizzly, just larger due to their salmon diet.) From the safety of elevated viewing platforms, visitors can watch bears catching salmon as the fish valiantly leap over Brooks Falls. The downside of the park's popularity is that one will want to make reservations at least a year in advance if one hopes to stay at one of the cabins near the bear-viewing platforms, especially for the peak bear-viewing period of July. If July is not available, consider late June, August, and September. There may be fewer bears, but there will still be plenty to see and the crowds of people should be smaller. While it's perfectly rational to wonder about one's safety in the midst of so many large bears, the park has an exceptional safety record thanks in part to a requisite bear-safety course, safe bear-viewing platforms, a food-storage system, and diligent and knowledgeable rangers.

3 ⤳ May

Prairie Dogs of the Badlands

In the month of May the North American prairie comes alive. Larks and other birds have returned and are singing from sunup to sundown. Wildflowers are in full bloom, with new species emerging every day. And the butterflies and other pollinators are busy doing their priceless work. Far below ground in the deep, dark, prairie dog burrows the newborn black-tailed prairie dogs are getting restless. For weeks they've huddled together in their nests of grass, relying only on their senses of touch and smell to take in the cramped quarters around them. But on one magical day in May they make that long, unsure walk up the dark burrow and into the light of day. Imagine what that must be like. In one step they are entering a whole new world, and their wonderment shows as they explore and frolic on the vibrant prairie. At Badlands National Park in western South Dakota the wildlife observer gets to be a part of it.

What's Remarkable about Black-Tailed Prairie Dogs?

Every ecosystem seems to have a single species around which it revolves. For example, in streams and ponds the beaver is the ecosystem engineer that can literally change the habitat, affecting many other species. In the vast oceans the incredible swarms of krill are the biomass upon which many other species depend. And in the Pacific Northwest's rivers it's the salmon, a species that literally brings with it the nutrients of the ocean to

The prairie dog and its family, with the frolicking, curious, and playful young, is one of the prairie's most charismatic species. (Photo by Daniel S. Licht)

What is the most important species of the prairie ecosystem?

There's no easy answer to this question. One could argue that it's the microscopic fungi and other soil organisms that plants depend on. Perhaps it's the plants themselves as they are food, either directly or indirectly, for the animals. Or maybe it's the pollinators that the plants depend on. Regardless, what is undebatable is the importance of prairie dogs to the prairie ecosystem. Prairie dogs are what scientists call a "keystone" species. A keystone species is one whose presence influences a whole bunch of other species. Prairie dogs do that by providing prey for predators, excavating burrows that other animals use, recycling soil material and nutrients, changing vegetation structure and composition, and providing a variety of other ecosystem services. It's not an overstatement to say that you can't truly have a healthy prairie landscape without having a healthy prairie dog population.

the uplands. In the North American prairie, the black-tailed prairie dog is at the center of the ecosystem and is the species upon which much of the prairie's biological diversity depends.

Black-tailed prairie dogs are critical to a healthy prairie landscape. They engineer habitat by digging burrows that often become homes for other animals. They are an abundant and reliable food source for coyotes, eagles, badgers, ferrets, and many other prairie species. And they consume vast amounts of vegetation, converting it into nutrient-rich fertilizer that they deposit above- and belowground. Their digging cultivates the soil so that seeds may germinate. So important is the black-tailed prairie dog in the health of a prairie ecosystem that the species may be the epitome of a "keystone species."

Prairie Dog Behavior

Prairie dogs are, of course, not actually dogs, but rather a kind of ground squirrel found only in North America. They were given the name of prairie "dog" by early Great Plains explorers in reference to their constant barking at the explorers or any other potential danger.

Of all the adaptations that prairie dogs possess, their communal lifestyle is their key to survival. These social creatures live in "towns" that historically covered many, and sometimes hundreds, of square miles. The Great Plains—as are grasslands throughout the world—are conducive for social animals. The bountiful and nutritious forage allows animals to live in close proximity to one another, and the high visibility allows individuals

A prairie dog giving the "yip" call, the primary use of which seems to be an "all clear" signal. Prairie dogs have complex societies, making them fascinating subjects for scientists and wildlife watchers. (Photo by Daniel S. Licht)

to keep tabs on what other group members are doing. It's no coincidence that gregarious animals, such as prairie dogs, bison, and pronghorn antelope, are mostly found in the open grasslands of North America.

Prairie dogs fascinate scientists in part because they are social animals, as we are. Family members and neighbors regularly communicate with one another. Their chirps and calls may sound like gibberish to the untrained, but science has found that they represent one of the more intricate languages in the animal kingdom. For example, some scientists believe that prairie dogs have different warning calls for different types of predators. Within the black-tailed prairie dog "town" there may be several different "wards." Think of the wards as different boroughs or municipalities in a large city. Individuals usually stay within their ward, but occasionally they move to another ward or perhaps even another town, sometimes only temporarily, sometimes permanently. Prairie dog families, known as coteries, raise their young, warn each other of danger, play and frolic, and yes, sometimes even fight among themselves. Prairie dog society is so interesting and complex that entire books have been written about the subject.

Yet this idyllic scene is not all that it appears. Danger lurks everywhere in the form of coyotes, bobcats, black-footed ferrets, badgers, swift fox, golden eagles, ferruginous hawks, red-tailed hawks, rattlesnakes, and many other species. Hence, one of the more obvious benefits of group living is that there are many more eyes and ears to keep a lookout for danger. All those eyes and ears make it extremely difficult for predators to take prairie dogs. Prairie dogs in the interior of the colony are especially well protected; animals on the periphery will sound the alarm at the first sighting of danger. Not surprisingly, studies have shown that individuals in the interior of the colony have higher survival rates. Yet there are trade-offs. Prairie dogs in the most desirable portions of the town must defend their turf from other prairie dogs. Tempers can run high, especially during the February breeding season when the males fight for turf and for females. Aggression can also turn deadly once the young are born; infanticide is believed to be a significant mortality factor. How a species can be loving and protective of its own kind and yet at other times commit atrocious acts of infanticide is just one of the many reasons why prairie dogs are so intriguing to scientists.

Prairie Dog Conservation

Conservation of the prairie dog, and especially the black-tailed prairie dog, has not been easy. In pre-Columbian times the black-tailed prairie dog likely numbered in the billions, with some prairie dog towns covering hundreds of square miles. But farmers and ranchers have despised the prairie dog since they first sunk a plow or pounded a fencepost into the Great Plains, so they conducted massive poisoning programs. Farmers and ranchers believe that prairie dogs eat vegetation that could be going to their cattle, and they accuse prairie dogs of being a destroyer of range-land. Yet the thirty million or so bison that inhabited the pre-Columbian Great Plains showed just the opposite as they prospered and proliferated on the same prairies that also supported billions of prairie dogs. Science has begun to unravel how that is possible.

The relationship between prairie dogs and bison is complex, but consider just one aspect of the story. Most grasses and forbs sprout, grow, flower, seed, and die in just a few months, at which point the plants no

Prairie dog grazing helps keep the prairie landscape healthy. (Photo by Daniel S. Licht)

longer provide quality forage for herbivores. In the prairie, most plants grow in the spring and dry up in the summer. However, if the plants are clipped in the growing or flowering phase they may start over, even if it's late in the season. If they're clipped again, they try again to complete all their life phases. This means the plants will stay vibrant, green, and nutritious well into the summer. That is what prairie dogs do; their constant clipping of plants keeps the vegetation constantly growing. If a landscape consists of a patchwork of prairie dog towns intermixed with areas without prairie dogs it creates a diversity of vegetation conditions, which is ideal for bison as there is diversity and foraging choices on the landscape. The bison simply move to the habitat type that offers the best foraging at that time of the year.

Interestingly, bison also benefit prairie dogs. Prairie dogs do not like tall vegetation because it makes it harder for them to see predators, and therefore they will not colonize such areas. However, bison grazing and trampling can convert tall vegetation into short vegetation, making the site more conducive to prairie dog colonization. The established prairie dogs then begin clipping the vegetation, which creates better forage for bison. Bison and prairie dogs are forever linked on the Great Plains in a relationship that scientists call mutualism (i.e., a symbiotic relationship in which both species benefit).

In spite of prairie dogs' ecological benefits, the species continues to be persecuted, especially on private lands. That is why national park units are so important to the conservation of the species. Parks are one of the few land ownerships where prairie dogs find protection. Regrettably, there are only a few national parks within the historic range of the black-tailed prairie dog, and those that do exist are only of modest size.

Parks with Prairie Dogs

Badlands National Park, South Dakota

Traveling on Interstate 90 across the Great Plains of South Dakota it is impossible to miss the distant peaks of the badlands puncturing the otherwise flat grassy landscape. The buttes, pinnacles, and walls dominate the horizon from miles away. Tan color during midday, at sunrise and sunset the yellow, ocher, orange, and other hues come out to the delight of the artist and photographer (especially after a summer rain). As the sun moves across the sky the long shadows the rugged topography create emphasize the three-dimensional world that stands in stark contrast to the surrounding plains. The badlands are an unforgettable landscape of ever-changing geologic formations and indefinable shapes created by the effects of rain, wind, temperature, and time. Although constantly changing (some of the peaks and spires may erode an inch or more a year), the landscape gives one the feeling of timelessness as if one has just stepped back hundreds of thousands of years (the fact that Pleistocene fossils may be at one's feet adds to this timelessness).

At the core of the badlands physiographic region is the 244,000-acre Badlands National Park. The park is divided into North and South Units. Most of the visitation occurs in the North Unit as it has much better access. The east portion of the North Unit gets the most visitors since the road there is blacktopped, the visitor center is there, and the badlands formations are most dramatic in that area. However, the best wildlife viewing is in the western half of the park, which is only accessible by the gravel-surfaced Sage Creek Road. In fact, the bison are only found in the western half of the North Unit. Although prairie dogs can be found in both the east and west halves of the unit, the largest colonies are in the west half.

As with most national parks, Badlands National Park has a well-developed system of excellent hiking trails. All of the trails will take a visitor through some "out-of-this-world" scenery. The best time to hike is early morning when the temperatures are pleasant, the wildlife is most active, and the badlands topography is most colorful. Regardless of when one hikes or the length of the trail, bringing water is a necessity as the summer sun can dehydrate a person in a hurry and there is no potable water in the park. Also, keep an eye out for prairie rattlesnakes (yes, they are dangerous, but we view an encounter with a rattlesnake as a positive experience; these fascinating creatures are an important part of the prairie wildlife community).

We strongly encourage visitors to Badlands National Park to spend a night or two camping to best experience the essence of the prairie ecosystem. The region is ideal for camping; it is mostly bug free, the nighttime sky is amazing, and the nighttime temperatures in May are perfect for

Badlands National Park consists of rugged badlands topography intermingled with mixed-grass prairies. (Photo by Daniel S. Licht)

sleeping. For those wanting to be closer to amenities there is a campground near the park headquarters. For a more natural experience there is the Sage Creek drive-in campground at the west end of the park, bordering the Badlands Wilderness Area. At this campground one may wake up to a herd of bison milling around the tent as well as prairie dogs barking in the nearby town. If visitors want a camping spot all to themselves, they should take a short hike from that campground and enter the badlands wilderness where all that can be heard are coyotes serenading and the gentle breeze of a prairie night.

Prairie dogs are easy to see, perhaps more so than any other species featured in this book. In fact, seeing prairie dogs is every bit as certain as seeing mountains, caves, forts, and the other physical attractions found in parks. That's because prairie dogs live in towns and the towns don't go anywhere (at least not over short time spans). Badlands National Park supports about 7,000 acres of black-tailed prairie dogs and dozens of towns. Information available at the Cedar Pass Visitor Center at the east entrance to the park can provide the exact locations of the towns, many of which are bisected by the park's roads.

May is an especially exciting time to observe prairie dogs because it is the time of year when the newborn young first emerge aboveground. One can almost see the wonder and amazement in their eyes as they cautiously emerge from the darkness of their natal burrows and see for the first time the blue sky and green grass and hear the barking and yelping of hundreds of other prairie dogs. After absorbing their new world, testing their legs, tasting some plants, and pushing some dirt around, the young siblings may begin a wrestling match that can go on for an hour or more. One cannot help but be amused and entertained by this demonstration of youthful exuberance. The wildlife watcher will see sneak attacks as one sibling pounces on another and they both tumble down the side of the burrow mound. One will see them wrestle over a dry, worthless twig as if it was the most delicious morsel on earth. And one will see them yank, tug, and bite each other's tails, apparently not realizing that the tail is actually connected to a sibling.

MORE WILDLIFE IN A PRAIRIE DOG TOWN

The black-tailed prairie dog is considered a keystone species, meaning that it benefits many other species. Science has confirmed that the biological richness of prairie dog towns is typically much higher than the surrounding prairie (of course, both habitats contribute to the overall

In national parks prairie dogs are often tolerant of people, but as always, don't approach too closely and don't feed the wildlife. (Photo by Daniel S. Licht)

biodiversity of the prairie ecosystem). Look for these ten species (table 5) in a prairie dog town:

Table 5. Ten species found in the prairie dog ecosystem

Bison	Look at the prairie and where the bison are. They may be in the prairie dog town because the grass is often greener there.
Pronghorn	Prairie dog towns have more forbs than areas outside of the towns, hence pronghorn often feed in prairie dog towns.
Horned Lark	A songbird, they like the short/sparse vegetation found in prairie dog towns. Like many prairie birds, they nest on the ground.
Burrowing Owl	A family of burrowing owls perched on a prairie dog mound, looking inquisitively at you, is about as photogenic as it gets.
Coyote	The clever coyote has its wits tested when hunting prairie dogs, as a prairie dog will give the alarm call when it sees a coyote.
Badger	Perhaps the most feared predator of prairie dogs as they can dig prairie dogs out of their extensive burrow systems.
Golden Eagle	Although they nest in trees and cliffs far from the prairie dog town, they often fly to the towns to hunt prairie dogs.
Black Widow Spider	Famous because the females often eat the males after mating; look for their webs in abandoned prairie dog burrows.
Mountain Plover	Another endangered species that needs heavily grazed prairie, conditions created by prairie dogs.
Black-Footed Ferret	If you see one of these extremely rare nocturnal animals you've hit the jackpot. They are found only in prairie dog towns.

One of the more interesting and charming residents of prairie dog towns is the burrowing owl. This diminutive owl has adapted to life in the treeless Great Plains by using old prairie dog burrows for nesting. The birds lay their four to twelve eggs deep down in an abandoned burrow. When not incubating the subterranean eggs the adults often spend their time perched on prairie dog mounds. The most heavily used mounds will

Burrowing owls use prairie dog burrows for home, and they feed on the abundant prey in prairie dog towns. (Photo by Daniel S. Licht)

be marked with their "white-wash" droppings. The best time of day to see the owls is early morning and sunset, although they can be found in the middle of the day as well (another oddity of this owl; they are diurnal). If one is at a prairie dog colony in midsummer one may see a family of young burrowing owls lined up soldierlike on a mound, all owls staring at the visitor with their big, inquisitive eyes. The prairie dogs themselves have nothing to fear from the owls because the burrowing owl diet is comprised mainly of insects, mice and voles, small snakes, and other very small prey.

Other Parks with Prairie Dogs

At least twenty-one national park units support prairie dogs. Parks in the Great Plains have black-tailed prairie dogs whereas parks in the intermountain west typically have one of the other four species of prairie dogs. Black-tailed prairie dogs are by far the most abundant species, comprising about 83 percent of the 14,500 acres of prairie dogs on Park Service lands.

Wind Cave National Park, South Dakota
Wind Cave National Park is located on the southern edge of the Black Hills, only a two-hour drive from Badlands National Park. Although originally established to protect the namesake cave, the park also protects

28,000 acres of prairie and forest. This national park abuts Custer State Park, one of the largest state parks in the country. Although the two parks combined support only 4,000 acres of prairie dogs, it's enough prairie dogs to increase the biological diversity of the parks. For example, in 2007 Wind Cave National Park reintroduced the rare and critically endangered black-footed ferret. The nocturnal ferret is totally dependent on large prairie dog towns to survive. The park is the only place in the world that conducts regularly scheduled nighttime ranger-led walks looking for ferrets. Even if visitors do not see a ferret during these walks, they are sure to spotlight coyotes, bobcats, and other species that are active at night.

Devils Tower National Monument, Wyoming

The world-famous Devils Tower is forever ingrained in the public's psyche as a landing site for aliens (thanks to the movie *Close Encounters of the Third Kind*). But for more down-to-earth people it is the site of one of the more incredible geological marvels on earth, that being the huge igneous tower that rises 1,000 feet up from the otherwise rolling prairie and forests. Hundreds of thousands of people come from great distances every year to view the legendary tower. But what is the second most popular visitor attraction at the park? It's the 40-acre black-tailed prairie dog colony at the base of the tower. The colony is right next to the main park road and the National Park Service kindly puts up informational signs describing prairie dog ecology. The colony has apparently been at the site for at least a century as the reports and journals of early explorers made note of a prairie dog town at the base of the tower; hopefully, the colony will be there for centuries to come.

Theodore Roosevelt National Park, North Dakota

This park's rugged badlands topography was carved by the erosive power of the Little Missouri River and the labyrinth of stream channels that drain into it. Although prairie dogs have been extirpated from much of North Dakota, they find refuge in the park. However, the park does not contain the classic flat Great Plains prairie dog habitat; instead, the colonies are wedged into what little prairie there is between the buttes, hills, drainages, and other craggy topographic features. Fortunately for the wildlife observer, some colonies are adjacent to the main park road. There are several pull-outs that include interpretive displays about prairie dog ecology. The scenic park road also provides an opportunity to view bison, elk, pronghorn antelope, and other grassland wildlife. Many of these same large grazing mammals can also be seen at more famous parks such as Yellowstone, but at Theodore Roosevelt National Park one can see them without the crowds and traffic jams.

Bryce Canyon National Park, Utah

This 35,000-acre park supports the Utah prairie dog, a cousin of the black-tailed prairie dog and the most threatened of the five prairie dog species. The species had been extirpated from the park, so they were reintroduced in the 1970s. The reintroduction has been successful enough that park animals have been translocated to start other populations outside the park. About 300 acres of Utah prairie dog colonies currently exist in the park; however, these acres may support no more than three hundred individuals. But this is not untypical for this species of prairie dog. Utah prairie dogs live in very sparse and low-density colonies, a consequence of the sparse and slow-growing desertlike vegetation in the region. In fact, to the casual observer, Utah prairie dogs may not even seem colonial. Whereas the black-tailed prairie dogs in the forage-rich Great Plains may average twenty-five animals per acre, the Utah prairie dog may average only one animal per acre; there just is not that much food available. Keep in mind that the Utah prairie dog is a federally protected threatened species so do not disturb or harm them in any way (this should hold true for all park wildlife).

Dinosaur National Monument, Colorado–Utah

Dinosaur National Monument is home to the white-tailed prairie dog. Like the Utah prairie dog, white-tailed prairie dogs typically occur at low density. So even though the park has about 1,700 acres, they don't have nearly the abundance of animals that would be found in a black-tailed prairie dog town. In this desert landscape the prairie dogs are most active around sunrise and sunset as they try to avoid the midday heat. To help them survive the harsh winters, and the lack of forage available at that time, these prairie dogs hibernate, in contrast to black-tailed prairie dogs, which are active all winter long.

Summer

The Little Missouri River in Theodore Roosevelt National Park in North Dakota. This gem of a park gets relatively little congestion compared to Yellowstone and Yosemite, yet it also provides excellent wildlife-viewing opportunities. (Photo by Daniel S. Licht)

Summer is the season of peak visitation in most national parks. This is especially true in many of the more famous parks such as Yellowstone, Yosemite, and Shenandoah, where the campgrounds are full, visitor centers are crowded, and wildlife "jams" are frequent. Yet some great national park units are mostly undiscovered by the masses. In this section we focus on those parks, as we believe that the absence of crowds and quality wildlife viewing go hand in hand. Sociologists have noted that the quality of an outdoor experience is often correlated with how it differs from a person's everyday life. In other words, if a person spends most of his or her life in crowds and then goes to a crowded park, the experience will not seem that remarkable or different. However, if one escapes the masses and enjoys some quiet time in a less populated park the valuable vacation and outdoor experience will be of much higher quality, more memorable, and more rejuvenating.

In this section we highlight three wildlife species that could not be more different. In fact, about the only thing they have in common is that they are fascinating animals that occur in fascinating places. They also happen to be found in national park units that don't experience the crowds and congestions of some of the more famous units.

We start in June with sea turtles in the warm tropical waters of Dry Tortugas National Park, a boat ride away from the end of the Florida Keys. When people think "wildlife watching in national parks" they don't always include the underwater world, but they should. Anyone who can swim can snorkel, and those who snorkel enter a whole new environment. Watching a sea turtle effortlessly glide through aquamarine waters is an unforgettable experience. Seeing the diversity of colors and life found in the ocean need not be limited to nature shows on television, and it does not require expensive trips to faraway places. It can happen right here in the United States.

Summer—nature's paradox

We're not going to lie and tell you that summer is the perfect season for viewing wildlife. True, summer has a lot to offer, but there's also a lot to be aware of. For example, in some ecosystems the heat of summer sends the wildlife looking for cool shade, which they won't leave until nightfall. In other places summer is the height of the mosquito season. And summer is also a season of abundance so some animals are just plain lazy and inactive. But having said that, there is also a lot to see in summer, if you know where to go and what to look for. For example, if you want to hear the roar of the rutting bison, witness the perseverance of nesting sea turtles, or marvel at hundreds of thousands of bats in flight, you need to head out in summer.

In July we get about as far as one can from the ocean when we visit the heart of the Great Plains to view that iconic American species, the bison, also known as the buffalo (in the scientific world, bison is the correct name whereas buffalo refers to African animals such as the Cape buffalo). Theodore Roosevelt National Park in western North Dakota is not only a great place to view this symbol of the American West, it's also a fitting place to learn about their remarkable conservation story as that park's namesake played a leading role in saving the species. July is one of the best times to view bison because it is their mating season. At that time of the year the powerful bulls are in full glory as they roar, tear up the earth, and fight each other in battles that have been going on for millennia.

In August we travel to the desert Southwest to visit Carlsbad Caverns National Park. This may seem illogical (traveling to the desert in the middle of summer), but it is the best time to see one of nature's great spectacles, the hundreds of thousands of Brazilian free-tailed bats exiting the Carlsbad Caverns entrance as the sun sets over the desert. For the wildlife watcher the show is worth putting up with the midday heat. And, of course, when one wants to escape the heat it's always possible to feel the coolness of one of the world's great caves.

4 ⌣ June

Sea Turtles of the Dry Tortugas

There are few experiences as serene, as calm, and—somewhat paradoxically—as exhilarating as being underwater and watching a sea turtle effortlessly swimming through a turquoise sea. These animals exemplify peacefulness as they glide through an underwater world we can only visit. Of course, sea turtles are only one of many fascinating and colorful animals that can be found in the world's oceans. And nowhere are the oceans more alive and colorful than in the coral reef habitats. The healthiest and most colorful coral reefs in the contiguous forty-eight states are those found in Dry Tortugas National Park, an island park far off the Florida Keys. One needs a boat or floatplane to get there, but it's well worth the ride.

What's Remarkable about Sea Turtles?

The first sea turtles appeared on earth over 100 million years ago, at a time when the earth was populated with dinosaurs. Somehow these turtles survived the mass extinction event that killed off the dinosaurs and many other species about 65 million years ago. Although it's easy to say the turtles survived because they were in the oceans, that doesn't fully explain their persistence; many ocean "dinosaurs" such as plesiosaurs (not technically dinosaurs, but often lumped with them) and other sea creatures became extinct. In fact, it's been estimated that three-quarters of the species identified in the fossil record disappeared during that cataclysmic

Watching a sea turtle swim is almost surreal. At Dry Tortugas all one needs to see these creatures is a swim mask and snorkel. (Photo by Daniel S. Licht)

period (perhaps due to a massive meteorite hitting the earth). So how did a slow-moving, nonaggressive, cold-blooded animal manage to survive when so many others perished? It's a mystery that may never be solved, but what is known is that sea turtles are remarkable creatures.

Sea Turtle Species
There are five species of sea turtle in the Atlantic Ocean. The loggerhead and green sea turtles are the principle nesters along the beaches of the southeastern United States, with the loggerhead by far the most abundant (although that's a comparative description as they too are a threatened species). However, divers and snorkelers most frequently observe green sea turtles due to their strong fidelity to shallow coastal waters such as those at Dry Tortugas National Park.

LOGGERHEAD SEA TURTLES
Loggerheads are the most commonly observed nesting sea turtle, comprising 90 percent of the egg layers on Florida beaches. Every couple of

Against all odds

Seeing a sea turtle in its natural environment is an unforgettable moment as you watch the animal swim with ease through its underwater environment. It seems to have such a trouble-free life, but think about this. That sea turtle is one in a thousand. When it hatched many years prior it was just one hatchling among many in that nest, and that nest was one of many on that beach, and that beach was one of many beaches. That turtle you are looking at made it to adulthood, either through luck, skill, or most likely, a combination of both. Meanwhile, 999 other hatchlings didn't survive. Some never got out of the egg, some never made it out of the nest, some never survived the journey down to the water's edge, some perished shortly after entering the ocean, and many others died as juveniles while out in the vast ocean.

years egg-bearing females migrate to their natal beaches where they laboriously crawl up the beach, excavate a 20-inch-deep hole in the sand, and lay their fifty to two hundred eggs. About two months later, usually under the cover of darkness, the eggs hatch and the young dig their way out of the sand and make their perilous journey down the beach and into the sea. The lucky ones that make it to the ocean adopt a drifting lifestyle at the mercy of the currents. The young turtles feed on tiny marine animals found in the wandering rafts of seaweed. Once the turtles reach the size of a dinner plate they feed mostly on shellfish. Eventually, the turtles will mate and the females will make their epic journey to the same sandy beaches where they were born to continue the circle of life.

GREEN SEA TURTLES

Green sea turtles are the quintessential herbivore in the shallow estuaries where they graze on what is commonly referred to as turtle grass. Somewhat paradoxically, this grazing keeps the grass beds healthy because the clipped vegetation grows more vigorously after it has been grazed. This is not unlike the impact of prairie dogs and bison on the grasslands of the Great Plains. Green sea turtles are the species most frequently observed by snorkelers and divers. They can be seen at Dry Tortugas National Park as well as Key Biscayne and Virgin Islands National Parks and at Kaloko-Honokohau National Historic Park in Hawai'i.

KEMP'S RIDLEY SEA TURTLES

Kemp's ridley sea turtles (also known as Atlantic ridley sea turtles) are the smallest sea turtle as well as the most endangered. Juveniles feed on anything from worms to shellfish, but when adult they feed primarily on crabs. Synchronized waves of females come ashore to nest on beaches at Padre Island National Seashore in Texas and at Playa de Rancho Nuevo Sanctuary in Mexico. The related olive ridley sea turtle is found in the Pacific Ocean and is believed to occasionally show up at Point Reyes National Seashore and Redwood National Park.

HAWKSBILL SEA TURTLES

Hawksbill sea turtles use their unique hooked bill to feed on the hard crusted sponges that make up their primary prey. This long-lived sea turtle does not migrate as widely as other species, spending most of its life near tropical coral reefs and nesting on islands scattered throughout the Caribbean. The hawksbill's distinct shell has a central keel and serrated edges, making it easy to recognize and the source of the term "tortoise" shell. Unfortunately, the beautiful dark-patterned shell made it a target of shell hunters to the point that the species was extirpated in some places. The species is considered uncommon or occasional in park units.

LEATHERBACK SEA TURTLES

Leatherback sea turtles belong to their own taxonomic family. These monsters can attain a length of 6 feet and weigh in at 1,400 pounds. As the name implies, they have a thick, leathery skin on their back versus a hard shell like the other sea turtle species. They are amazingly well adapted to the deep open ocean and are capable of diving deeper than any other air-breathing reptiles (up to 3,200 feet). This ancient turtle's unique ability to generate its own body heat allows the turtle to travel to

A hawksbill sea turtle. (Photo by Paul Brown)

the cool waters of the North Atlantic. Scientists speculate that some dinosaurs may have shared this trait. The species is not considered common in any park units.

Sea Turtle Conservation

In historic times sea turtles likely numbered over 100 million individuals. Sadly, all five species of Atlantic sea turtles are now listed as threatened or endangered under the Endangered Species Act, with the leatherback, Kemp's ridley, and hawksbill being critically endangered. It's a commentary on our rapidly changing world that creatures that have persisted for 100 million years can suddenly find their future in jeopardy. Fortunately, their plight is well known and conservation measures are being undertaken.

The decline in Atlantic sea turtles began almost as soon as European explorers discovered the animals. In short time sea turtles were overharvested everywhere and totally extirpated from islands like Jamaica and the Caymans. Although harvesting sea turtles for food is now almost universally prohibited, animals are still collected illegally as part of the black market trade in wildlife parts. This problem appears to be especially severe in portions of Central America and the Pacific Islands. In addition to illegal harvest, sea turtles now face other threats to their existence. One such threat is that sea turtles get entangled and drowned in commercial

Park rangers assisting a turtle hatching along a popular beach. (Courtesy National Park Service)

fishing nets in what is known as *bycatch* (species caught that are not the intended target). New gear and better enforcement has reduced this mortality factor, but not completely. For example, shrimp fishermen in the Gulf of Mexico now use "turtle excluder devices" that reduce the bycatch of sea turtles by 97 percent, but the loss of even a few individuals can be harmful to turtle populations.

Another huge concern is the loss of the critical beach-nesting habitat. In some cases direct destruction or alteration of sandy beaches has occurred as new condos, hotels, and other structures are built. In other cases it's the high amount of recreational use by people and their pets that impacts the nesting turtles. Another issue is light pollution on the nesting beaches. Turtle hatchlings appear to use the moon to navigate toward the ocean, but bright artificial lights can lure the hatchlings the wrong direction, that is, away from the ocean.

Pollution continues to be a worldwide problem impacting sea turtles. The Gulf of Mexico oil spill of 2010 degraded marine habitat, although quantifying such impact on sea turtle populations is always difficult. Perhaps the biggest impact to sea turtles is yet to come. Climate change threatens to degrade the coral reefs that sea turtles and many other species depend on. Climate change may also impact sea turtles indirectly by making them more vulnerable to disease, pollution, and other impacts.

As a result of the precipitous decline in sea turtle numbers, extreme conservation measures have been taken to restore populations. For example, until recent times tens of thousands of Kemp's ridley sea turtles came ashore at Playa de Rancho Nuevo, Mexico, to nest, but by 1980 fewer than four hundred females nested there. The United States and Mexican governments formed a compact to save the species. Over 22,000 turtle eggs were collected from Mexico and shipped to Padre Island, Texas, for care and incubation. The captive-reared hatchlings were then released on Padre Island beaches and allowed to temporarily enter the surf to imprint the smells and other characteristics of the site. The young turtles were then taken to Galveston, Texas, and raised in captivity for another year to increase their odds of survival. The yearlings were then finally released

Sea turtle hatchlings heading toward the ocean. Only about one in a thousand will survive long enough to reproduce. (Courtesy National Park Service)

into the wild. Some of the captive-raised turtles have survived to adulthood and have returned to Padre Island to lay their eggs.

Parks with Sea Turtles

Dry Tortugas National Park, Florida

Located in the Caribbean, about 70 miles east of Key West, the island park is actually closer to Cuba than the US mainland. To get to the park one takes a boat or seaplane from the Florida Keys. The centerpiece of the park is Fort Jefferson on Garden Key, an unfinished military fort started in 1846 (comprised of sixteen million bricks, it is the largest masonry structure in the Western Hemisphere). The word *dry* in the park's name refers to the lack of fresh water on the islands. The word *tortugas* comes from the Spanish explorer Ponce de León, who visited the site around 1513; he saw an abundance of *tortugas* (sea turtles) and supposedly killed 160 of them. Fortunately, sea turtles are now protected from harvest, and they are once again common in the park waters.

With 99.8 percent of the 101-square-mile park being water, this is truly a marine park. The site is world famous among ecologists and conservationists and has been designated an International Biosphere Reserve. In 2007 a new layer of protection was added as a 46-square-mile Research Natural Area was established within the park boundary (the largest designated area in the lower forty-eight states). Within this area no fishing or

A boat is needed to get to Dry Tortugas National Park, but once there the bird watching and snorkeling is amazing. (Courtesy National Park Service)

A young sea turtle at Dry Tortugas National Park. (Courtesy National Park Service)

other harvest is allowed and boats are not allowed to anchor, all in an effort to better protect the marine ecosystem. Research areas are of enormous value to scientists as they provide a baseline by which to compare other areas that may be impacted by human uses.

Dry Tortugas National Park is seven small islands far out in the vast Gulf of Mexico. Therefore, the park doesn't provide a lot of the outdoor activities found in other park units, such as auto tours, backcountry hiking, horseback riding, and such. In fact, the park doesn't even provide the normal amenities such as food, water, and shelter. However, the island park does provide one very unique outdoor activity: camping on an ocean island. There is a primitive campground on Garden Key, just outside of the walls of Fort Jefferson. At night, sitting outside a tent, the visitor will hear only the waves of the ocean and the sounds of the nesting birds on nearby Bush Key. In the dark night sky above one will see a million stars, free of the light pollution that occurs on the mainland. Camping also allows one to enjoy the island for longer than the three to four hours the commercial ferries allow. Another option for a multiday visit is to spend a night or two in the vicinity of the islands on a live-onboard vessel. One will still hear the waves and birds and see the stars, but will have a soft bed and a cold drink should they be desired. In addition to the fort, another significant cultural resource at the park is the three hundred or so shipwrecks in the waters around the park. One will need to dive into the water to see most of these, but some, like the Brick Wreck, are only a few feet deep and easily visible from a boat. Artifacts, like coral and other natural resources, are of course protected within all national park boundaries, so only pictures and memories may be taken.

All five species of Atlantic sea turtles have been documented at the park, with the loggerhead, hawksbill, and green sea turtles being most prevalent. Every summer some turtles venture up on the island beaches to bury their eggs. Scientists have attached GPS devices to some of these turtles to better understand their oceanic movements. What they have found is that the sea turtles that nest at Dry Tortugas are international travelers, moving throughout the Caribbean and Atlantic Ocean. The data demonstrates how important this tiny little speck of land is to wildlife throughout the region. While there is never a guarantee that one will see a sea turtle, Dry Tortugas National Park provides an excellent opportunity.

MORE WILDLIFE AT DRY TORTUGAS NATIONAL PARK

Perhaps more so than any other park, the three systems of land, water, and air come together at Dry Tortugas National Park. The meeting of these three systems means the park is rich in biological diversity and is excellent for wildlife watching. The marine environment supports over three hundred species of tropical fish and countless species of invertebrates. Much of the richness depends on healthy coral reefs. Coral is made up of countless tiny organisms known as polyps; the polyps join together and secrete a calcium shell that forms a skeleton. Over thousands of years a reef develops from these skeletons. Sea turtles make use of these valuable habitats. Some, like green sea turtles, actually help maintain the

Sea turtles affixed with GPS devices at Dry Tortugas travel great distances. (Data courtesy US Geological Survey)

health of the reefs because they feed on the algae that could otherwise damage coral.

Upon landing at Garden Key, what is most noticeable to the visitor is the overwhelming loud squawking and screeching of tens of thousands of birds, many of which nest on the tiny islands (table 6). June is the peak of this cacophony as the recently hatched chicks and juveniles join the adult birds. Most of the birds nest on the mostly treeless Bush Key, which is within earshot of Fort Jefferson on Garden Key. The sooty terns, with their provocative calls and ritualistic displays, are one of the more notice-able and entertaining species. Approximately 30,000 sooty terns nest at

Dry Tortugas, the only regular nesting site for the species within the United States.

The most unmistakable seabird found in south Florida is the magnificent frigate bird. Dry Tortugas National Park supports the largest gathering of these birds in North America. This conspicuous bird really stands out during its courtship ritual when it inflates its red throat pouch as if it were a balloon. Their flight is equally as impressive as they soar over the ocean in search of food. They can remain airborne for days, simply coasting on warm updrafts (these updrafts are often associated with approaching weather fronts so experienced sailors would monitor frigate birds for changing weather). Yet for a bird with an 8-foot wingspan they are also surprisingly maneuverable as they scoop up surface-swimming fish, squid, and even the occasional sea turtle hatchling. Frigate birds also go by the name "man-of-war" as they often steal or "pirate" the prey of other birds. In some cases frigate birds may harass a bird so that the victimized bird regurgitates its meal, which the frigate bird then happily consumes.

More Parks with Sea Turtles

The various sea turtle species can be found in almost any park unit that includes tropical waters, such as those in the Caribbean and Hawai'i, and even some parks in more temperate waters. Green sea turtles occur in the most parks, being present or probably present in twenty-five units. Eighteen units report the presence of leatherbacks, sixteen units report loggerheads, ten parks report hawksbills, and nine report the presence of Kemp's ridley sea turtles.

Gulf Islands National Seashore, Mississippi and Florida
In 2005 the islands were completely inundated by Hurricane Katrina. Yet life returned. In 2010 the islands took the brunt of the Gulf oil spill. In spite of the tens of thousands of person hours spent cleaning the beaches, oil continues to wash up on shore or be exposed by the shifting beach sands. Yet the health of the ecosystem will eventually return, as will the sea turtles. Some of the park's barrier islands—comprised of sparkling

Table 6. Ten species to see in the marine-beach ecosystem

Magnificent Frigate Bird	About 100 of these magnificent birds nest on Long Key, the only known nesting colony in the continental United States.
White-Tailed Tropic Bird	A seabird that can be found throughout the world, it is notable by its very long central tail feathers.
Goliath Grouper	A large fish that can weigh hundreds of pounds; they tolerate people, making them a favorite of snorkelers and divers.
Brown Noddy	These international birds are found all over the world. About 4,500 nest on Bush Key and can be seen with binoculars.
Sooty Tern	They nest on Bush Key. That key is closed to visitors, but the birds can be seen from Garden Key.
Coral	Park has about 30 kinds. Hard corals literally build the reefs. Elkhorn and staghorn corals are threatened species.
Brown Pelican	Now common, they are one of a few species that recovered to the point of being removed from the endangered list.
Masked Booby	These uncommon birds plunge almost vertically and at high speed into the water for prey.
Angelfish	There are many colorful kinds. Their flat shape helps them navigate and, if necessary, hide in the coral.
Barracuda	Odds of seeing this ocean predator while snorkeling the Keys are good. Don't worry, there is little to fear.

Nesting magnificent frigate birds. (Courtesy National Park Service)

white sand and sparse beach vegetation—require a boat to get to, whereas others can be reached via car. Regardless of the vehicle, the destination is well worth the time.

Biscayne National Park, Florida

Ninety-five percent marine, this is the largest marine park in the National Park System. Much of the shoreline habitat within the park is comprised of mangrove forests, but there are some stretches of sandy beach used by nesting loggerhead sea turtles and the occasional hawksbill. Biscayne National Park is within sight of Miami, thereby offering easily accessible opportunities for city residents to observe sea turtles in a protected marine environment. Like most national park units, the park has an active volunteer program, including a program that uses volunteers to restore beach habitat and to monitor sea turtle nesting sites.

Canaveral National Seashore, Florida

This national seashore protects the longest pristine stretch of beach (24 miles long) in Florida. Here, Atlantic waves break on important nesting beaches for loggerhead and green sea turtles, all within sight of spacecraft

If one can swim one can snorkel. And snorkeling over a coral reef is just like the nature shows on television, only better. (Courtesy National Park Service)

Snorkeling and scuba diving are both natural and cultural experiences as fish and other marine life often congregate near old shipwrecks. (Courtesy National Park Service)

launching pads. Cape Canaveral is synonymous with space-age technology, so most people are surprised to find that the site also includes a protected natural ecosystem. Canaveral is a day-use-only park, which helps reduce disturbance to nesting sea turtles as most nesting activity occurs at night. There is, however, one way to visit the seashore at night; that is, to sign up for a scheduled guided nature walk. During June and July park naturalists guide small groups of visitors on nighttime "turtle watch" treks. It is the only authorized way to watch sea turtles crawl up on beaches to lay their eggs. In the 1980s scientists learned that predators destroyed over 98 percent of the park's turtle nests each year, so park rangers and volunteers work each night to place wire-mesh cages over the nests to protect them from predators. (Predation by raccoons and other predators may seem like a natural process; however, many of these predators are far more abundant now than they would be under natural conditions due to human activities such as leaving garbage and food on the beaches.)

Padre Island National Seashore, Texas

This national seashore protects the longest undeveloped stretch (over 70 miles) of barrier islands in the world. These windswept islands are constantly changing as violent hurricanes create storm surges that reshape the sand dunes. The white sand is ideal for sea turtles looking for warm beaches to deposit their eggs. Because the beaches are also popular with recreationists the park staff and volunteer "beach patrols" drive the beaches looking for nesting Kemp's ridley sea turtles or signs of their nests (in contrast with other sea turtles, Kemp's ridley sea turtles often nest during the day). If a sea turtle is spotted, an "alert flag" is raised on the beach to warn vehicles to slow down and watch out for nesting turtles. In some cases eggs are collected and the young are raised in captivity. When the captive hatchlings are released back into the wild the public is invited to watch the release, a way to build public support for the program (contact the park for more information). In 2010, over five thousand people watched twenty-three turtle release events.

5   July

American Bison of Theodore Roosevelt

"We landed, ascended the bank, and entered a small skirting of trees and shrubs that separated the river from an extensive plain. On gaining a view of it, such a scene opened to us as will fall to the lot of few travelers to witness. This plain was literally covered with buffaloes as far as we could see, and we soon discovered that it consisted in part of females. The males were fighting in every direction, with a fury which I have never seen paralleled, each having singled out his antagonist. We judged that the number must have amounted to some thousands, and that there were many hundreds of these battles going on at the same time . . . I shall only observe farther, that the noise occasioned by the trampling and bellowing was far beyond description. In the evening, before we encamped, another immense herd made its appearance, running along the bluffs at full speed, and although at least a mile from us, we could distinctly hear the sound of their feet, which resembled distant thunder."

The explorer John Bradbury wrote the above account during his travels through the Great Plains around 1810. We may never again witness such a scene on the same scale as Bradbury, but bison can still be seen, their powerful battles still witnessed, and their thunder still heard. One of the best places to see this iconic species is Theodore Roosevelt National Park

There are few animals as powerful or as dangerous as a bison bull during the summer rut. (Photo by Daniel S. Licht)

in western North Dakota. This park is an appropriate place to discuss bison as its namesake played a critical role in the conservation of the species.

What's Remarkable about American Bison?

As recently as 15,000 years ago, mammoths, mastodons, camels, oxen, horses, and various species of bison roamed the vast grassy plains of North America. With the exception of the plains bison, all of these species went extinct around 10,000 years ago (scientists have several theories for this mass extinction, including overkill by the first humans to North America). It's the American bison, *Bison bison,* that survived and prospered while the other large beasts perished. From Arctic-like blizzards of winter to the scorching heat and dryness of summer, from packs of wolves to grizzly bears, from ancient hunters to modern-day threats, the bison perseveres, a testament to luck, adaptation, and grit.

Bison Behavior

The roar of the rutting bull bison is one of nature's most powerful sounds. It rumbles across the prairie landscape announcing to all that the bison mating season has returned to the Great Plains. A large herd of bison, consisting of numerous bellowing bulls, can be heard for a mile or more (the greenhorn will often think it's thunder, even though there be not a cloud in sight). For most of the year the cows and young animals travel together in moderately sized herds, while the bulls are off by themselves in small bachelor groups. But come July the mature bulls join the cow herds for the mating season. The bulls don't defend a territory or group of cows, but rather, a cow that is ready to mate. As one looks at the herd of bison one will see bulls standing closely alongside cows. If the cow tries to leave, the bull may shepherd or turn her in a different direction. This "dance" will continue for as long as she is in estrus. During that twenty-four hour period he will have to fend off all suitors. If a weaker bull approaches he will chase it off, but he needs to be careful because other bulls may "steal" the cow while he's preoccupied; if a larger bull approaches he may concede the cow and head off looking for a new

The bison is the symbol of the Department of the Interior, the department that the National Park System resides in. (Photo by Daniel S. Licht)

female. But if the two bulls are equally matched a fight may break out—two of nature's most powerful contestants in a battle that literally stirs the earth. Hair, vegetation, and dirt fly as two tons of power and fury collide in combat under the sweltering summer sun. The fights may last only a few seconds, with one violent butting of heads clearly settling the dispute, or they may go on for many minutes. The longer fights seem to attract the attention of the rest of the herd, as if they know they are witnessing an epic struggle. At the conclusion of the summer breeding season all of the receptive cows will have bred, but only the most powerful bulls (or rarely, a sneaky bull) will have passed their genes on to future generations.

Although the American bison is sometimes called "buffalo," that name is scientifically incorrect as the term *buffalo* more accurately refers to the

The plains bison was the staple of the Plains Indians. Their entire existence re-volved around the bison. (Photo by Daniel S. Licht)

Asian and African water buffalo. The plains bison is an incredibly well-adapted animal. Consider that it must withstand the scorching sun and parched prairie of summer, with temperatures exceeding 100 degrees Fahrenheit, and then just a few months later the animal must endure the deep snow, blinding blizzards, and 40-below windchills of a Northern Great Plains winter. The bison survives these weather extremes not by flying south, or hibernating in a hole, or even huddling together en masse, but rather, by simply standing out in the open and taking nature head-on. Perhaps even more amazing is that the breeding season of the bison—a period when the bulls are most stressed from the almost constant bellowing, fighting, and mating—occurs under the sweltering sun of the Great Plains summer. Such timing seems a poor adaptation, but it's necessary so that the calves can be born the following spring just as the lush green grasses are peaking.

CAUTION—BISON ARE DANGEROUS!

It may surprise some that this apparently docile herbivore would harm people, but the truth is that wild bison may be the most dangerous animal most park visitors will encounter. Bulls weigh up to a ton and cows weigh half that, and both sexes can run as fast as a horse. They can use their hooves, head, and horns to hurt people (the same tools they use to fight off grizzly bears, packs of wolves, and mountain lions). At Yellowstone National Park bison have actually injured more people over the past several decades than bears, wolves, coyotes, bobcats, and mountain lions combined. Bison are especially dangerous during two behavioral periods. One is the calf-rearing season, which usually begins in early May and gradually tapers off throughout the summer and early fall. Cows will aggressively protect their calves from all potential predators, including people. It's extremely dangerous for any predator to be between a cow and her young calf. In fact, even if you are not between the cow and calf you may still be at risk as cows sometimes lose sight of their calves and may panic and become aggressive when they see a potential predator.

The second high-risk behavioral period is during the mating season (i.e., rut), which occurs from mid-July to mid-August. At this time the testosterone level in bulls is peaking and the animals are extremely belligerent and aggressive. Although most of the hostility is aimed at other

Caution

Do Not Approach Bison

Bison are wild animals and best viewed at a distance.

This sign may look funny, but it's deadly serious. Bison are likely responsible for more human injuries in parks than bears, mountain lions, and other predators combined. (Photo by Gary W. Vequist)

bulls, it could quickly and unexpectedly be aimed at a nearby person. One warning sign to look for is the position of the bison's tail. A tail raised straight up could indicate that the bison is agitated by the presence of a person and anyone present should quickly back off (a raised tail could also indicate a sexually aroused animal—in neither case does one want to be too close). If the bison becomes even more alarmed or agitated at human presence it may bluff charge and/or stomp both front feet (note that this is not always preceded by the raised tail warning). Quickly back off. Although every situation is different, a good rule of thumb is to get no closer than 50 yards to a bison and always be aware of escape options.

Bison Conservation

The American "buffalo" has become the symbol of the American West, both its past, its present, and its future. The conservation story of the plains bison has no equal. Prior to European settlement there may have been fifteen to thirty million bison in North America, with most of them roaming across the vast Great Plains. Within just a few short decades in the middle of the nineteenth century the species was almost extirpated: the result of a vicious slaughter for hides and meat, for sport hunting, and in an effort to remove the primary food source of the native Indians. By the mid-1880s just a few hundred animals existed, found in zoos, a few small private herds, and the remote reaches of Yellowstone National Park. The most prominent wildlife species in North America—and the symbol of the Department of the Interior (the department that includes the National Park Service)—had essentially been eliminated from the earth.

But thanks to a small handful of visionary conservationists the restoration and recovery of the bison soon began. Bison were afforded protection in Yellowstone National Park. Animals from that herd were soon used to stock other parks and refuges. Eventually, animals would be returned to Indian reservations and private lands. By some counts there are now about five hundred thousand bison in North America (however, only ten thousand or so are on public lands with the rest being in managed private herds). Bison are now raised on private ranches and marketed for their healthy meat, valuable leather, and other commercial products. The future of the bison looks bright, but there are still a few

The future looks good for the American bison, thanks in part to national parks. (Photo by Daniel S. Licht)

clouds on the horizon. For example, many bison in private herds contain cattle genes, a consequence of past attempts to crossbreed a more adaptable livestock on the Great Plains. The National Park Service and other federal agencies are taking steps to conserve the genetically "pure" bison. Another problem with current bison management is that there are no large bison herds roaming the Great Plains exposed to wolves and bears, the natural predators that historically kept the bison herds fit and healthy. As a result of this missing natural process, the less fit bison are now more likely to pass their harmful genes to future generations. Still, the future for bison looks much brighter than it did a century ago.

Parks with Bison

Theodore Roosevelt National Park, North Dakota

Located in western North Dakota, this park is named in honor of the twenty-sixth president of the United States who came to the region to hunt buffalo and left as a conservationist. The park is one of the lesser visited but more surprising and spectacular parks in the National Park System. After driving for hours through flat Northern Great Plains rangeland and farmland the visitor suddenly comes upon a rugged byzantine landscape carved out of the prairie plateau, something akin to a Grand Canyon in the Northern Great Plains.

The park is actually split into two primary units known as the North and South Units, each about 30,000 acres in size. The South Unit receives most of the visitor use because it is conveniently located along Interstate 94 next to the town of Medora, a tiny "western" community that in the summer hosts a professional musical, small shops, a museum, and other items with an American West theme. The South Unit also has a slightly larger and much more visible bison herd.

The park has many of the amenities of most national park units. Especially noteworthy is the excellent hiking through the beautiful badlands scenery. However, before venturing off on a hike bring a good map and compass or GPS unit as the established hiking trails can sometimes become confused with well-worn bison trails, and one wrong turn can get a hiker lost in the complex maze of canyons, draws, walls, and buttes (the established hiking trails are marked with signs that have a logo of Theodore Roosevelt wearing a bow tie, which can, under the shimmering summer sun, start to look like a skull and crossbones). The park is also excellent for horseback riding and has commercial operations in the park for dudes. Riding a horse can re-create Theodore Roosevelt's experiences.

As is the case in many parks, Theodore Roosevelt National Park has a "wildlife loop" road in the South Unit of the park. It can be traversed in one hour, but a visitor should really plan for a half a day. The three hundred or so bison in the South Unit can be seen almost anywhere along the road in the small patches of mixed grass prairie habitat intermingled among the buttes, cliffs, draws, and other badlands topography. However,

Theodore Roosevelt National Park in western North Dakota was the home for its namesake prior to his becoming president. It's fitting that a park with bison be named after him as he played a key role in the conservation of the species. (Photo by Daniel S. Licht)

Kids are natural outdoor explorers. All they need is a parent to give them the opportunity. (Photo by Daniel S. Licht)

in July the bison are usually found in the prairie dog towns where the road parallels the Little Missouri River. Keep in mind that July is the mating season and the bison are dangerous (in fact, park rangers may ticket you if you get too close to bison).

The more remote North Unit also has bison; however, the blacktop road into the unit dead ends so one has to come out the same way one got in. Also, the bison tend to be less visible along the road than they are in the South Unit.

MORE WILDLIFE AT "HOME ON THE RANGE"

Although bison are found in a variety of habitats, they reached their greatest abundance on the vast grasslands of the North American Great Plains. The wide-open spaces are also where the deer and the antelope roam, as well as many other animals (table 7). During a summer day exploring the North American prairie, try to find these grassland species:

What's the fastest animal on earth?

It depends on how you phrase the question. Although the cheetah is typically given the title of fastest land animal, it depends on
the distance, because once you get past 100 yards the cheetah
fades while the North American pronghorn antelope is still going
strong. In fact, if the race is over 200 yards then the pronghorn
takes the title of fastest land animal! These speedsters have top
speeds of 55–60 miles per hour, about 15–25 miles per hour
faster than their main predators, the coyote and wolf. So why is
the pronghorn so absurdly fast compared to the predators it must
evade? One hypothesis is that the pronghorn evolved on the
North American plains along with the North American cheetah;
however, the latter went extinct about 13,000 years ago. Yet
even after the extinction of the North American cheetah the
pronghorn has retained its amazing speed.

The pronghorn antelope is the fastest mammal in North America and worldwide
may be second only to the African cheetah. (Photo by Daniel S. Licht)

Table 7. Ten iconic prairie species

Bison	The iconic animal. The bison represents the American West, the prairie ecosystem, government agencies, currency, sports teams, etc.
Pronghorn	The prairie speedster. Look through your binoculars. Your vision is now comparable to the vision of the pronghorn.
Elk	Most people think of elk as mountainous species, but they are really more at home on the grassy prairies.
Prairie Dog	Spend some time watching this critter as you will see them play, fight, bond, communicate, and perform many other behaviors.
Coyote	One of nature's ultimate survivors, coyotes are found in many habitats such as the wide-open prairie.
Meadowlark	The songster of the prairie, these yellow-breasted birds continue singing every morning well into midsummer.
Ferruginous Hawk	Early explorers often called this bird the "prairie eagle" due in part to its large size. They often nest on the ground.
Sharp-Tailed Grouse	The "sharpie" and its cousin, the prairie chicken, are famous for their group dancing displays in April–May.
Swift Fox	This cat-size fox needs habitats with short vegetation and lots of burrows so it can see and escape from predators.
Dung Beetle	Watching a pair of dung beetles roll and push a fecal pellet larger than they are symbolizes parenthood everywhere.

If the bison is the iconic large mammal of the Great Plains, then the pronghorn deserves second place. With its binocular-like vision, its herding behavior, and its incredible speed, this ungulate is ideally suited for the vast grasslands. Pronghorns are so well suited for running they actually have nine different gaits, ranging from a walk to a full rotary gallop. Although often called the pronghorn "antelope," the North America pronghorn is not a true antelope, but rather a distinct species belonging to a taxonomic family of which it is the last surviving member (the pronghorn's closest surviving relatives are in the giraffe family). The "prongs" of the pronghorn's horns and the fact that the horns' outer sheaths are shed annually are two characteristics that set the pronghorn apart from true antelopes found in Africa and other parts of the world. Like the American bison, the pronghorn is a survivor, and in the case of the pronghorn, it truly is the last of its kind.

Other Parks with Bison

Ten units report having bison, but in a couple of those units the bison are actually on non–Park Service lands within the park boundary (e.g., bison at the Niobrara National Wildlife Refuge within the Niobrara National Scenic River).

Tallgrass Prairie National Preserve, Kansas

This preserve contains some of the best remaining remnants of a once vast tallgrass prairie ecosystem. This ecosystem of waist-high big blue-stem, switchgrass, and Indiangrass once extended from Manitoba south to Texas, but being such fertile land it was quickly and almost completely broken up and destroyed by the plow. However, the tallgrass prairie in the Flint Hills of Kansas overlays bedrock only a few inches below the surface, making the land impervious to the plow. Most of the region is currently used for ranching, but the Tallgrass Prairie National Preserve near Cottonwood generates tourism dollars for the community. In 2009 the park introduced a small herd of bison transplanted from Wind Cave National Park. For the first time in 150 years the eastern Kansas landscape now includes active bison wallows (large depressions in the earth made by bison; they sometimes take on the characteristics of very small wetlands, increasing biodiversity). Visitors can now see bison walking through the chest-high grasses, colorful wildflowers, vociferous songbirds, and myriad butterflies that call the tallgrass prairie home. The park provides a free prairie bus tour from the historic Springhill Ranch to the hilltops that overlook the prairie where bison roam once again.

Badlands National Park, South Dakota

Perhaps no park comes closer to displaying bison in their classic Great Plains habitat than does Badlands National Park in western South Dakota. At the park the bison can flex their legs and wander across a 64,000-acre wilderness area, a large portion of which is rolling prairie ecosystem. The only way to see the bison is to drive the dirt road through the western half of the park. Regrettably, many visitors don't take this road as they stay on the main east–west blacktop road. Taking the dirt road not only allows the westbound visitor to see bison, it's also a scenic and convenient

A herd of bison grazing at Badlands National Park, much like bison have for millennia. (Photo by Daniel S. Licht)

route to Highway 44, which heads to Rapid City and the beautiful Black Hills. For a unique and memorable experience visitors should consider camping at the Sage Creek Primitive campground on the edge of the wilderness area. There is a very good chance that campers will wake to a herd of bison grazing outside their tent.

Wind Cave National Park, South Dakota

Although originally established in 1903 to protect the namesake cave, the park was soon expanded for purposes of being a "game preserve" to conserve the dwindling populations of bison, elk, pronghorn antelope, and deer. Next to Yellowstone, it is probably the most important National Park System unit in terms of bison conservation. The park now conserves such a wide diversity of large mammals that it has sometimes been called a "Little Yellowstone." In fact, the park is the only site in the world that contains bison, elk, pronghorn antelope, prairie dog, and black-footed ferret, all representative mammals of the grassland ecosystem. A drive on the main north–south highway through the park will almost guarantee a chance to see bison; if not, take the dirt road in the east half of the park for a quieter bison-viewing experience.

Yellowstone National Park, Wyoming

Yellowstone protected the only remaining herd of wild plains bison at the end of the nineteenth century. This priceless herd was fundamental to saving the species, as some of Yellowstone's bison were transplanted to Wind Cave, Badlands, and Theodore Roosevelt National Parks as well as other sites. Today there are three thousand bison within the park's 2.2 million acres. The best places to see bison are the Lamar and Hayden Valleys; however, keep in mind that bison are nomadic. This means that where they are today they may not be tomorrow. What makes Yellowstone bison viewing exceptional is that the animals are exposed to the full range of natural predators, including wolves and grizzly bears. With patience, persistence, and a little luck one may observe bison fending off, or falling prey to, wolves and grizzly bears much like they've been doing for millennia.

6   August

Bats in Carlsbad Caverns

The sweltering desert landscape of the American Southwest may not seem like an ideal wildlife-watching destination in August. But within the caves at Carlsbad Caverns National Park in New Mexico the temperatures can run 20–40 degrees cooler than the outside desert. That cool subterranean climate is ideal for the hundreds of thousands of Brazilian (a.k.a. Mexican) free-tailed bats that roost in the caves during the day. Come evening the bats awake and leave the cave in a mass exodus as they venture out into the desert to feed. Watching swarm after swarm of bats corkscrew their way up into the fading twilight and then depart toward the distant horizon is one of nature's great wildlife-viewing spectacles.

What's Remarkable about Brazilian Free-Tailed Bats?

Every summer evening since time immemorial a half-million or so Brazilian free-tailed bats exit Carlsbad Caverns to head out into the surrounding desert to feed. Upon leaving the cave the "clouds" of bats—yes, that is one of the terms for a group of bats—corkscrew upward into the evening sky in a counterclockwise pattern. Why counterclockwise? Some have speculated that this behavior is due to the Coriolis effect, the same earthly phenomenon that causes the water in your bathtub to drain in a counterclockwise pattern (assuming you live in the Northern Hemisphere). Although the Coriolis effect is extremely weak, a bat trying to gain altitude needs all the assistance it can get, so the ascending bats

Brazilian free-tailed bats leaving Carlsbad Caverns for their nighttime foraging. (Photo by Nickolay Hristov)

may use it to more efficiently ascend. This counterclockwise pattern is so ingrained in bats they even use it in confined spaces such as inside houses. When the Carlsbad Caverns bats return to the cave at the end of the night they don't need this earthly assistance to descend so they simply dive in a straight line into the cave entrance.

How are bats similar to butterflies?

Starting in August huge numbers of recently hatched monarch butterflies migrate south from the central United States and Canada to the forested mountains of Mexico. Likewise, many species of bats also migrate to Mexico for the winter, including millions of Brazilian free-tailed bats that summer in and near US national parks. Fortunately, Mexico has established reserves and protected areas for these winter residents. As bats and butterflies both demonstrate, species conservation is often an international affair requiring protected areas and national parks on both sides of a border.

Bat Echolocation

In the blackness of a cave or on a moonless night eyesight is of little value to a flying bat. Therefore, bats have developed the fascinating skill of using echolocation to navigate and hunt. A bat emits a series of high-frequency clicks, inaudible to us. These high-frequency sounds bounce off objects in the bat's flight path and are reflected back to the bat's ears. The bat's ears send the signals to the brain, which creates a virtual image of what's in front of the bat. Of course this all happens almost instantly. In order to zero in on flying insects—the prey for most North American bat species—the clicking pulses the bat emits become more rapid and the pitch becomes higher. This echolocation, combined with the bat's maneuverability, makes the bat a lethal predator of flying insects. By the time the night is over the insectivorous bat may have consumed over 50 percent of its own weight in bugs. Multiply that by the hundreds of thousands of bats exiting Carlsbad Caverns and that is a lot of free insect control.

Bat Conservation

As we continue to learn more about the mysterious lives of bats we realize just how vulnerable they are to man-made hazards. For example, it appears that many insect-eating bats suffered greatly from widespread pesticide use during the 1950s and 1960s. Fortunately, with better testing and regulation, pesticides are no longer a severe threat. An ongoing threat is cave disturbance. Careless or malicious people entering a cave can disturb bats, thereby causing the bats to leave their young, utilize precious energy reserves, and sometimes even abandon the cave. A relatively new threat to bats is wind turbines, which are popping up all over the country to generate electricity. Bats are amazing nighttime flyers, but they haven't yet been able to avoid the whirling blades of a wind turbine farm. Researchers are looking into ways to promote this renewable energy source while minimizing its impact on bats. However, the greatest future risk to bats appears to be a new disease known as white-nose syndrome. This disease has killed millions of cave-dwelling bats in the eastern United States and Canada. Worse yet, this fungal disease appears to be rapidly spreading to caves in the southeast and central United States and perhaps eventually, to caves throughout North America. There are many unknowns about the disease, including how it spreads, but transmission by people moving between caves is a possibility. Hence, National Park Service managers are beginning to grapple with the difficult decision of how and when, or even whether they should, allow people into caves. It's an extremely difficult decision as several park units—such as Carlsbad Caverns National Park—were established in large part for purposes of cave recreation and visitation.

Parks with Brazilian Free-Tailed Bats

Carlsbad Caverns National Park, New Mexico

About 400,000 visitors enjoy Carlsbad Caverns National Park year-round. Most visitors come to see the park's famous cave system. The 117 known caves contain some of the largest rooms of any caves in North America, many of which are connected by a spectacular underground labyrinth of tunnels, openings, and other features. However, the park is much more than just caves. Aboveground is the rugged yet beautiful Chihuahuan Desert wilderness.

There are several excellent hiking trails in the park. Adjacent to the visitor center and the cave entrances is the Desert Nature Trail that takes one by yuccas, junipers, and other desert plants. Other longer hiking trails take one into the desert backcountry. Water and safety gear is, of course, a must for any backcountry hiking. To truly appreciate the desert one must spend some time out and about at night. Carlsbad Caverns National Park does not have established campgrounds, but backcountry camping is allowed. The park also conducts several nighttime "Star Party" events where telescopes are provided for viewing stars and planets. Here, away from the light pollution of the cities, one can make out the countless constellations of the night sky.

There are many other natural wonders and things to see at Carlsbad Caverns National Park, perhaps the most amazing being the twilight flight of hundreds of thousands of bats from the park's caverns. Every summer evening for time immemorial the bats have amazed wildlife watchers. Legend has it that a pioneer cowboy decided to investigate the site where Carlsbad Caverns National Park now stands when he saw a large, dark mass rising up from the ground and corkscrewing into the evening sky. He originally thought it might have been a volcano or whirlwind. It was, of course, the exodus of thousands, if not hundreds of thousands, of Brazilian free-tailed bats from what would become known as Carlsbad Caverns. In addition to the abundant Brazilian free-tailed bat, there are at least sixteen other bat species that live in the park.

As dusk approaches hundreds of people arrive at the large cave entrance to witness the bat exodus. The park has built a beautiful outdoor amphitheater to accommodate the wildlife watchers. Perched on rock benches at the cave entrance, spectators wait in eager anticipation for the first bats to emerge. While they patiently wait, a park naturalist describes bat ecology and conservation. Inevitably, the setting sun brings the first bats from the cave entrance (technically, nobody knows what cue the bats use to leave the dark depths of the cave). The audience suddenly becomes silent as the first bats emerge, first by the handfuls, then by the hundreds, and then by the thousands. The bats circle upward, whirling and rising, silhouetted against the twilight sky. Then the swarms level off and head toward the horizon and into the darkness. After the show, which can last one to several hours, visitors head back to their rooms to sleep while the bats busily feast on the insect population for miles around.

As morning approaches the bats return to the cave. Some bats return at night, whereas many others come at dawn or even during daylight. The

Visitors gathering for the evening spectacle of thousands of bats leaving the cave. (Photo by Gary W. Vequist)

amphitheater is open to anyone who chooses to return in the cool morning hours to witness the return. In contrast to the evening flight, the returning bats fly directly over the cave entrance, fold back their wings, and dive into the cave at 60 mph, disappearing into the darkness. The vanishing of the bats is soon followed by the always-spectacular desert sunrise. As if that wasn't enough for the wildlife watcher, a new event soon begins. From the same entrance where the bats disappeared, hundreds of cave swallows emerge to begin their daytime insect feeding. The morning ritual is often observed by only a few people, but for those who want a little more guidance or company in watching the bats return in the morning, the park hosts a morning "bat flight breakfast" once a year in July or August.

MORE DESERT WILDLIFE

Carlsbad Caverns National Park is a great place to view a diversity of desert wildlife in addition to the bats. One can encounter the better-known residents (lizards, snakes, and tarantulas) along with a few surprises like firefly larvae (glowworms). An especially good place to view wildlife at the park, even in the middle of the summer, is Rattlesnake Springs, an oasis of life in the desert. Here one can watch and listen to an assortment of birds, mammals, and frogs. The site is so popular it has been called the unofficial birding capital of New Mexico. See table 8 for desert wildlife to look for at the park:

Table 8. Ten desert species to look for

Texas Banded Gecko	Deserts are known for their reptiles. The Texas banded gecko is primarily a nocturnal species.
Brazilian Free-Tailed Bat	What Carlsbad Caverns is famous for. The exact population size is unknown, but it may be in the hundreds of thousands.
Black-Chinned Hummingbird	Ten different species of hummingbird have been found in the vicinity of Carlsbad Caverns, including the black-chinned.
Ringtail	A lot of desert species come out only at night. The ringtail—a relative of the raccoon—is one such nocturnal species.
Chihuahuan Spotted Whiptail	Whiptail lizards fascinate scientists because some populations are all female and have asexual reproduction.
Collared Peccary	Not a true pig, peccaries are social animals that often form small herds.
Harris's Hawk	Somewhat rare in the park, this species is known for its unique cooperative or pack-hunting behavior.
Greater Roadrunner	Roadrunners—a member of the cuckoo family—can run up to 20 miles per hour.
Turkey Vulture	Circling vultures are a symbol of the hot scorching desert and of death (although they circle for other reasons as well).
Western Diamondback Rattlesnake	Another symbol of the West, one tends to find them when not looking for them!

One of the "poster" species of the desert Southwest is the greater roadrunner, a member of the cuckoo family. This odd bird is easily recognized with its long tail, spiked head feathers, and quirky mannerisms. Although roadrunners can fly, they prefer to stay on the ground using their impres-

The roadrunner is one of the iconic species of the desert Southwest. (Photo by Daniel S. Licht)

sive speed (estimated at 20 mph) and agility to catch prey (e.g., lizards, snakes, and insects).

Whereas the roadrunner prefers the warm daylight hours (they may even go into a slight torpor during the cool desert night), many other desert species mostly or only come out at night. One such species is the kangaroo rat. This small mammal is so well adapted to the dry desert that it gets all the water it needs from the seeds and plants it eats. The kidneys of this desert specialist are so powerful at recycling moisture the animal is known to "urinate" what are essentially solid crystals of bodily waste.

Other Parks with Bats

Bats are ubiquitous throughout North America, although in northern parks they may only be present or active in the summer months. Many of the best units for year-round bat viewing are located in the desert Southwest.

Cave swallows nesting on ledges near a cave entrance. The Carlsbad Caverns population may be the best-studied colony in the world as the park has been studying them since 1980. (Photo by Gary W. Vequist)

Bandelier National Monument, New Mexico
Twelve species of bats including the Brazilian free-tailed bat are found in this monument. In summer many of the bats inhabit the walls of the numerous canyons in the park, including the popular Frijoles Canyon. This canyon also contains a number of ancestral pueblo homes and other cultural resources dating from the AD 1100–1600 era. The park is extremely popular with hikers as it has over 70 miles of trails through some spectacular scenery.

Big Bend National Park, Texas
This huge desert park is a long way from civilization and is definitely a place of extremes with scorching hot deserts and cool mountains. Named after the "Big Bend" in the Rio Grande, this 800,000-acre park has plenty of room to roam. The mountains, canyons, desert, and banks of the Rio Grande support a diverse assemblage of mammals, birds, and reptiles. Over twenty species of bats reside in the park, including Brazilian free-tailed bats. Bird watching is very popular in the park with over 450 species recorded, including some species found nowhere else in the United States. Although the park may support only a couple dozen cougars (a.k.a. mountain lions), the number of sightings is relatively high. Not surprisingly, this vast and diverse wilderness is an International Biosphere Reserve.

The collared peccary, also known as the javelina, survives in the harsh desert environment. (Photo by Daniel S. Licht)

Organ Pipe Cactus National Monument, Arizona

The 330,000-acre monument shares a border with Mexico and was set aside in part to preserve a unique cactus called the organ pipe. The park is at the northern end of the cacti's range; to survive in the "frigid" Arizona desert the plant is mostly found on warmer south-facing slopes. In spring the musky sweet perfume of the plant's white creamy flowers attracts pollinating bats. As the summer progresses the bats return to feast on the fertile fruits. Of course, to catch a glimpse of the bats one will need to be out in the evening. The park is so ecologically important and diverse that it too was established as an International Biosphere Reserve.

Saguaro National Park, Arizona

This park near Tucson protects the famous saguaro cactus, an iconic species known for its outreaching branches (arms). Every year when the cacti begin to flower thousands of endangered lesser long-nosed bats travel to the park to feed on the nectar. The next time visitors spot a cactus flower, they should think bats!

Chiricahua National Monument, Arizona

This monument conserves a mountain surrounded by desert lowlands. The park includes nineteen bat species in all shapes and sizes, including the Mexican long-tongued bat. As the name implies, that bat has a long tongue tipped with bristles for lapping nectar from agave flowers (also known as the "century plant," although technically they appear to only live ten to thirty years).

Fall

Fall brings some of the year's most exhilarating wildlife-viewing opportunities. In some places, such as the deciduous forests of the Midwest and New England, fall comes with a burst of color as leaves turn golden yellow, brilliant orange, and deep scarlet, providing a picturesque backdrop for wildlife viewing. Fall is the time of year when many wildlife species, such as the beaver, are busy collecting and storing food in anticipation of the long, lean winter months. However, other species are not focused on preparing for the coming winter. Rather, species such as elk are preoccupied with sex. Their bugles and clash of antlers echo across the forests, mountains, and prairies. In the Pacific Northwest salmon are also preoccupied with mating and perpetuating the species, but for them it will be the end of their journey. Once they deposit their eggs and sperm they will die, never to see the coming winter; however, their progeny will and the cycle of life will continue. Although the three species featured in the next three chapters are dramatically different in form and function, they are similar in that autumn is a critical season for the survival of their species.

Each September, Pacific salmon return by the tens of thousands to

Fall is the mating season for most large ungulates, making it an exciting time to visit national parks. (Photo by Daniel S. Licht)

Olympic National Park streams to spawn. Wildlife observers cannot only witness this timeless spectacle, as the salmon fight their way upstream, they can also see the many species of wildlife that depend on the returning salmon.

America's national parks are renowned for their large mammals, with the fall rut of the elk being a featured attraction in many parks, so much so that some parks have "elk jams." But there are lesser-known parks where elk can be observed in a less congested setting, such as at Buffalo National River in Arkansas. The bugle of the bull elk, a clarion challenge to other bulls and an enticement to cows, is one of the iconic songs of autumn.

Another autumn signature is the telltale *v*-shaped wake of a beaver swimming across a pond as it busily collects branches for its winter food cache. Cuyahoga National Park in Ohio, just south of Cleveland, is an unexpected place to see these industrious animals. And where there are beaver, there are often herons, ducks, mink, and all the other wildlife that call a beaver pond home.

Fall—the changing of seasons, and years

Fall marks the beginning of the end of the current year, but ironically it also marks the beginning of the coming year. It's the season when many animals from elk to salmon are thinking about procreating. Other animals, such as the beaver, are busy collecting food that will get them through the long winter and into next spring. Whereas summer allows for loitering and slumber, and winter sometimes requires it, for many species there is little time to rest in autumn. And that is why the wildlife watcher shouldn't rest either. Fall is one of the most exciting times of the year. Add to that a backdrop of brilliant fall foliage and brisk temperatures and you have a season you cannot miss. Fall is spectacular, but alas, it goes by in the wink of an eye.

7 September

Pacific Salmon of the Olympics

An adage attributed to Chief Seattle goes, "all things are connected, this we know." Perhaps no animal epitomizes this connectivity more than the five species of salmon. They start their life as small fry far inland in tiny freshwater streams. At this stage of their life much of the food they feed on comes, either directly or indirectly, from the surrounding uplands. After a year or so they migrate downstream to the vast ocean where they wander far and wide. Eventually, they return inland to the same streams

Salmon pair on a redd, a term for the gravel bed where the eggs are deposited. (Photo by Jon Preston)

where they were born to deposit their eggs, continuing the cycle of life. That is where they die, their bodies often being consumed by bears, eagles, and other terrestrial animals. At places like Olympic National Park in Washington the wildlife observer can see not only the salmon but also many of the other species that depend on the salmon's cycle of life.

What's Remarkable about Pacific Salmon?

Hundreds of streams on the West Coast empty into the Pacific Ocean. Almost all are potential salmon spawning habitats. Remarkably, when it's time to reproduce the pelagic (ocean-going) salmon—some of which may be several years old and thousands of miles from their natal stream—find their way back across the vast ocean to the very stream in which they started their life. How do they accomplish this incredible feat? Science appears to have unraveled the mystery—salmon use the distinct odor of the stream they were born in to navigate back to it. Even though they were only small fish when they left the stream, and it occurred several years prior, the scent is imprinted in their brain. The ability of these fish, which have spent their entire adult life in the ocean, to find their way back by scent to the very stream where they were born is truly a remarkable feat.

Salmon Ecology

There are five species of salmon in the Pacific Northwest: the chinook (a.k.a. king), coho (a.k.a. silver), pink (a.k.a. humpback), chum (a.k.a. dog), and sockeye (a.k.a. red). All are anadromous—meaning the adults return from the sea to ascend inland rivers to breed (anadromous comes from the Greek word for "running upward"). Their life begins when they hatch in the cold oxygen-rich waters of western streams. The newborn salmon are referred to as "fry." When they get larger they are called fingerlings (no exact criteria here; they are given that name when they get to— that's right—"finger size"). And when the young salmon head downstream to the ocean they are given the moniker "smolts." By now one may be wondering "why so many names?" Part of the reason is that the salmon's life is one of change—change in habitats, change in size, shape, and color.

Salmon and other fish are critical to Pacific Northwest ecosystems as they literally bring nutrients from the sea to inland waterways. (Photo by Gordon Dietzman)

In the vast ocean salmon may travel far and wide. Some salmon from North American streams have been documented as far away as the waters of Asia. After a few years at sea they are fully grown and ready to reproduce, so they make the incredible journey across thousands of miles of open ocean to arrive at their natal freshwater stream. Once they reach the freshwater streams the adult salmon stop eating and undergo a striking physical transformation. Coho salmon lose most of their silver coloration and change to a dull blue green. Pink salmon grow a hooked jaw and a hump on the back (hence their alias, "humpback"). Sockeye salmon turn a brilliant red (hence their alias, "red salmon"). In all species the immune systems shut down and the salmon are soon ravaged by all kinds of pathogens, resulting in a ragged appearance.

To reach the spawning grounds salmon often have to navigate past obstacles such as rapids, waterfalls, and shallow water, all the while avoiding a gauntlet of predators. By the time they reach the spawning grounds the salmon are physically exhausted and their fat reserves are gone. They are near death. Yet before their life ends they manage to start new life as they deposit their eggs in a bed of gravel known as a "redd," continuing the timeless cycle of the species.

The death of the spawning salmon is a gift to the same stream that gave the salmon life several years prior, and to the surrounding uplands that nourished it in its infancy. The salmons' decomposing carcasses return essential nutrients to the stream. The nutrients, either directly or indirectly, feed the next generation of young "fry" salmon. The salmon carcasses also provide an important food source for eagles, river otters, bears, and other wildlife. Pacific salmon are considered a keystone species and have been shown to directly benefit over eighty different birds and forty different mammals.

Salmon Conservation

Historically, the river systems of the Pacific Northwest supported unfathomable numbers of salmon. For example, the Columbia River Basin once sustained an annual run of twelve million wild salmon. Regrettably, those days appear to be gone forever. Numerous factors are responsible for the

The Elwha River cascades unimpeded from its headwaters in the Olympic Mountains until it runs into two downstream hydroelectric dams built almost a century ago. In a landmark decision, Congress directed the National Park Service to restore the Elwha River to a free-flowing condition, requiring the removal of the two dams. The goal is to restore the riverine habitat and the 400,000 salmon that once spawned in the river (currently only 3,000 salmon use the river). The dam removal project will reopen 70 miles of the river to spawning salmon (currently only 5 miles are available). For the local communities, this project is an investment in the future by restoring a priceless river ecosystem. The result will be increased tourism, recreation, and economic benefits. On a broader scale, the project will show what is possible for restoring salmon and riverine systems.

decline. Historically, overharvesting depleted many salmon stocks. The construction of dams and other obstacles to spawning habitat completely extirpated some salmon runs. For example, dams on the Snake River were an insurmountable barrier to salmon attempting to reach upstream spawning sites in Idaho. Dams also stop natural river hydrology such as flood events. Floods are needed to scour the streambed and flush debris from the system. Without these floods the gravel spawning sites become covered in silt and other debris. In addition to dams, the cumulative impact of logging, mining, and agriculture take a toll on salmon by degrading water quality in the streams. Water diversion from the streams for municipal and agricultural use also has had a harmful impact, directly and indirectly.

The recovery and conservation of salmon populations often requires a combination of sustainable harvests, habitat improvements, and removal of dams and other barriers. Progress is being made. For example, in some places dams are being removed in an effort to restore salmon habitat. Salmon recovery also requires a healthy ocean ecosystem. Salmon, as much as any other species, are affirmation of the idea that "all things in nature are connected." Not only do salmon connect ecosystems, they also connect human culture and history; the five species of Pacific salmon are the social and cultural foundation of many Pacific Northwest communities and Indian tribes.

Parks with Salmon

Olympic National Park, Washington

Over three million people visit Olympic National Park each year, but the park doesn't seem crowded because the visitors spread out into the park's various ecosystems, which range from snow-capped mountains to dry western conifer forests to deep, dark rain forests to ocean shorelines. At the center of the park are the Olympic Mountains and the headwaters for the numerous streams that flow north, east, and west to the sea. The cold, clear streams and rivers are ideal habitat for young salmon. As the waters flow past banks of maples, alders, and dogwoods the fallen leaves from the trees decompose in the streams, providing nutrients for aquatic invertebrates. These small organisms then become food for fingerling salmon. The fingerling salmon are food for otters, kingfisher, and other wildlife and the land and the stream become one interwoven ecosystem. Downstream, the river and the ocean meet, with the salmon moving back and forth between the two systems, and therefore land, river, and ocean are all connected.

The coastal rain forest ecosystem comprises a large portion of the Olympic Peninsula and is the signature ecosystem for the park. This rain forest habitat receives an incredible 12 feet (140 to 180 inches) of rainfall annually. However, September is a relatively dry month, with "only" 5 inches of rain. It is no wonder that water defines this place, whether it is a downpour, an ocean mist, or a turbulent stream. Unlike plants in the dry deserts, plants here do not compete for water—there is plenty of moisture. Instead, the competition is for sunlight. Trees reach for the sky, many growing hundreds of feet tall. Below the forest canopy ferns and herbaceous plants have evolved to survive on what little sunlight reaches the forest floor.

There is no shortage of things to do at Olympic National Park, ranging

A Pacific Northwest rain forest. Note the large trees, ferns, and various levels of decay and rot. (Photo by Gary W. Vequist)

from scaling snow-capped mountains to hiking foggy rain forests to taking idyllic walks on ocean beaches. The Olympic Scenic Loop (Highway 101) encircles the park. To truly see all that Olympic has to offer, visitors should plan on three to four days to circumnavigate the park and take in all the spur roads, trails, and overlooks. The Olympic National Park Visitor Center, located in Port Angeles, Washington, is the primary visitor center for the park and the only one open year-round.

We recommend starting your outdoor adventure there, as the park staff can provide all the information one needs regarding auto touring, hiking, camping, and wildlife watching. This is especially important as the park experiences frequent inclement weather, including unrelenting rains, deep snow, and dense fog. Keep in mind that starting in September some roads and campgrounds may be closed for the season. On the bright side, the first-come, first-served policy that can be problematic in summer is less likely to be so in the fall.

All five species of Pacific salmon can be found at Olympic National Park. The peak salmon spawning is in September; however, every species has its own timing, and some species have multiple runs so spawning salmon can be found almost any time from late spring to early winter. Highlights for the five species are:

CHUM SALMON

The park population of this species was dramatically reduced with construction of the Elwha Dams. They can still be found in the Queets and Quillayute Rivers in the summer-fall.

COHO SALMON

Perhaps the most popular species in the park, they have a summer and fall run. They are well known in the Sol Duc River, where they famously try to leap over the cascading falls.

SOCKEYE SALMON

The bright red body and blue heads of the spawning sockeye make them easily recognizable. They are found in the Quinault and Ozette drainages. The population that uses the Ozette is listed as threatened under the Endangered Species Act.

PINK SALMON

This species has its largest runs in odd-numbered years. Unfortunately, their numbers were greatly reduced by the construction of the Elwha Dams. They are often associated with the Dungeness watershed including the Gray Wolf River.

CHINOOK SALMON

Peak spawning is in the fall, but smaller spring and summer runs also occur. They can be found in all the park's coastal rivers and some tributaries. Prior to the construction of dams on the Elwha River some of these fish may have reached 100 pounds.

We recommend three sites to visit for viewing salmon. First, the Sol Duc River should be on a must-see salmon-viewing stop (the salmon enter this river via the Quillayute River). It is the only river in the peninsula that supports all five salmon species, and it also has a large run of steelhead trout (technically, they are rainbow trout that spend two to three years at sea before returning to freshwater to spawn). There are several sites on the river from which to view salmon, the most notable of which is the Salmon Cascades. An easily accessible crushed stone path leads from the Salmon Cascades Parking Area to a wood platform. At the platform one can watch salmon leap over the crest of the cascades. A few miles upstream of the Salmon Cascades viewing area is Sol Duc Falls—an impassable barrier to the salmon. A popular three-quarter-mile trail meanders past numerous salmon spawning beds on the way to these falls. Look for dorsal fins breaking the water surface as salmon swish the gravel to create their spawning beds. On this river coho salmon are completing their runs in September, whereas sockeye are more common in June and July.

The second place we recommend is the Hoh River, which cascades down past towering conifers on its journey to the sea. This swift-flowing glacier-fed stream is sometimes milky white with silt, but that does not deter the salmon from navigating upstream to spawn. Salmon often spawn later in the Hoh River, usually in November and December, but it's possible to see a few coho earlier in the fall. A good place to see salmon on this river is along the wheelchair accessible portion of the Hall of Mosses Trail at the Hoh Rain Forest Visitor Center (the center is only open on weekends outside the summer months).

The combination of marine, riverine, beach, and forest ecosystems makes the Pacific Northwest shoreline rich in biological diversity. (Photo by Gary W. Vequist)

The third site we recommend is the glacier-carved Quinault Lake, a 1,000-foot-deep lake cradled in the "valley of giants." At one time the sockeye salmon found in this legendary lake numbered in the millions; today fewer than five thousand salmon return. Nevertheless, it is still a good location to see salmon. Take the North Shore Road that leads to the upper Quinault River. In November-December sockeye salmon can be easily observed in the river.

As with all wildlife watching, practice good ethics and etiquette when watching salmon. At viewing platforms be considerate of others. And avoid walking in the streams as it's possible to step on a salmon redd and damage the eggs. One trick for enhanced salmon watching is to use polarized sunglasses to reduce the glare on the water surface (assuming the sun is out).

MORE WILDLIFE IN SALMON'S WATERSHED

Due to its variety of habitats, Olympic National Park is rich in wildlife diversity. In a single day one can, if lucky, see the endemic Olympic marmot in alpine areas, elk and spotted owls in forested areas, and orca whales from the ocean shoreline. During a day of exploring at Olympic

Table 9. Ten species found at Olympic National Park

Orca (Killer Whale)	Although uncommon, they are seen from the park's shorelines in summer and fall.
Gray Whale	More common than the orca, they can be seen from the park's shorelines.
American Dipper	A bird that literally walks underwater, the American dipper catches small invertebrates in the cold, clear streams.
Black Oystercatcher	Always found along shores, this all black bird with a long orange bill is easily identified.
Sea Otter	You'll find these charming animals off shore and their cousin, the river otter, in the park's rivers.
Banana Slug	One of nature's best recyclers, these "snails-without-a-shell" are found in the moist forest floor.
Harbor Seal	One of the more abundant marine mammals found near shore and a year-round resident at the park.
Olympic Marmot	Found nowhere else in the world, this social animal emits a high-pitched whistle when it spots danger.
Spotted Owl	Regardless of one's politics, it is undeniable that the spotted owl is a charismatic and photogenic species.
Roosevelt Elk	Also known as Olympic elk, the park was established in part for preservation of this subspecies of elk.

The dipper submerges its head and even walks underwater in search of aquatic insects. (Photo by Daniel S. Licht)

National Park try to find the animals (table 9) associated with the park's coastal, forest, and mountain environments.

A keen wildlife observer may spot a small, drab gray bird at home in the rushing streams of the park. The American dipper (also called a water ouzel) can often be seen on river boulders bobbing up and down. The bird then walks undeterred into the swift currents and disappears underwater. It walks submerged along the graveled river bottom using its especially large clingy feet to hang on to the substrate and its short wings to balance and propel it. Its water-repellent feathers shield it better than any raincoat could. While submerged it uses its bill to flip over small rocks looking for aquatic larvae hiding underneath. One can find these larvae (mayfly, caddis fly, stonefly, and midges) by turning over stones in the shallow waters (of course, return the rock to the same spot in the stream where it was found).

Other Parks with Salmon

Salmon are found in many parks near the Pacific Ocean. For example, chinook salmon are known from twenty-eight West Coast parks, including Alaska (as well as six Great Lakes parks where the species was introduced), coho salmon are known from twenty-five parks (plus six Great Lakes parks where the species was introduced), chum salmon are known from twenty-one parks, sockeye from twenty parks, and the pink from seventeen parks (plus two Great Lakes parks).

Redwood National Park, California
Redwood National Park's coastal streams flow under the stately grandeur of the world's tallest living things—the redwood trees. People come from all over to marvel at these two-thousand-year-old giants. A popular place to view salmon is Mill Creek near the town of Crescent City. A trail that follows the creek provides numerous salmon-watching opportunities. Farther down the coast, Redwood Creek once supported robust salmon populations, but these were severely diminished due to degraded water quality and quantity. Restoration is ongoing to improve the stream habitat so people can once again view spawning salmon.

Yes, the sign may appear humorous, but it is serious. Wildlife viewers need to always practice good ethics so they will be able to enjoy their activity in the future. (Photo by Gary W. Vequist)

Golden Gate National Recreation Area and the Muir Woods National Monument, California

These are two popular National Park Service sites near San Francisco. A fall run of coho salmon enters the Lagunitas River, which passes through Golden Gate National Recreation Area. Visit the Devils Gulch Trail and Shafter Bridge Fish Viewing Area for more opportunities to view spawning fish.

North Cascades and Mount Rainier National Parks, Washington

Both parks, located in the state of Washington, offer visitors the opportunity to view Pacific salmon. At North Cascades thousands of salmon work their way up the Skagit River from August to December. The spawning salmon, of course, attract an abundance of eagles, bears, and other wildlife. At Mount Rainier the Carbon River is the best place to see migrating salmon; the other major tributaries in the park all have downstream dams that block salmon migration (although some fish are transported around the dams).

8 ⌒ October

Elk of Buffalo River

In terms of photographic appeal there may be no animal in North America more sought after and more impressive than the North American elk in autumn. The adult males, known as bulls, carry their massive antlers proudly and regally. They use the enormous antlers to thrash small trees and to send clods of earth flying, all in an effort to demonstrate their fitness. Then they tilt the antlers back, extend their

Few animals are as majestic as the bull elk in the fall. (Photo by Daniel S. Licht)

head forward, and emit a loud buglelike call that carries for miles, as their breath turns to vapor in the crisp autumn air. And when two evenly matched bulls meet, an epic battle may ensue. For the photographer and wildlife observer it gets no better than elk in the fall. When most people think of elk they think of the Rocky Mountains, but surprisingly, there are many national parks outside of the Rocky Mountains where elk can be viewed. One of the better places to see these majestic animals in their fall glory is at Buffalo National River in the Ozarks of north-central Arkansas.

What's Remarkable about Elk?

Bull elk can weigh over 700 pounds, making them the second largest member of the deer family in North America (moose are the largest). However, what make elk stand out are their remarkable antlers. The antlers start growing in spring (as soon as last year's antlers are shed) and are fully developed by late summer–early fall. In large bulls the antlers can grow over an inch a day. Some claim that antlers grow faster than any other living tissue with the exception of some mushrooms. When fully developed the antlers on a large bull can weigh more than 40 pounds with the main beams exceeding 60 inches in length. To reach such an impressive size in such a short time a prime age bull needs lots of nutrient-rich food high in calcium and phosphate. Generally speaking, the size of the antlers is directly related to the health of the bull.

Unfortunately, in certain parts of the world some people believe elk antlers, like rhinoceros horns, bear gall bladders, and other animal parts, have special medicinal powers and therefore are smuggled and traded through the black market. Elk antlers are most valuable in the velvet stage when they are rapidly growing (there is some scientific evidence that antlers in this stage may indeed provide some physiological benefits to people in the form of growth stimulators and bone development). Hardened and shed antlers are often collected for decorative or craft purposes. However, collecting antlers is strictly forbidden in national parks in part because the shed antlers are part of the natural nutrient cycle. For example, many small rodents gnaw on the calcium-rich antlers.

Elk Behavior

For much of the year the adult bulls hang out in small groups known as "bachelor" groups while the cows, calves, and juveniles travel together in larger "cow herds." Come September the adult bulls join the cow herds in an attempt to gather a "harem" of cows for breeding. This breeding period is known as the "rut" (a term that apparently originated from early French or Latin words meaning "to roar"). The bulls advertize their presence and fitness by thrashing their antlers against vegetation, urinating frequently, and posturing. Perhaps the most striking breeding behavior is the bull elk's "bugle," a colloquial term for the high-pitched whistle the bulls produce. The bugle is often followed by a series of boisterous bellowing grunts. At the peak of the rut the bugling bulls can be heard day and night, although early morning is the peak period. The bugling, posturing, and thrashing of vegetation behavior not only proclaims the bull's

Hunting and national parks

It may surprise some, but many units the National Park Service manages allow hunting. Many of these units are designated as national lakeshores, seashores, preserves, and recreation areas. In contrast, units that have "park" in their name, such as Yellowstone National Park, typically do not allow hunting. Hunting can be an effective management tool to control populations of deer, elk, and other wildlife when natural predators are absent. However, hunting can also make the animals more fearful of humans and harder to see. Plus, many people do not want to be out recreating when hunters are present. This can create a dilemma for park managers. In some cases, such as Buffalo National River, the agency allows elk and deer hunting in most of the park, but there are areas where hunting is prohibited. These closed areas are popular with wildlife watchers because the animals are less likely to flee and the people can watch elk and other wildlife without fear of bullets flying by.

Fall is the mating season for elk. (Photo by Daniel S. Licht)

fitness to breed, it tells other bulls to back off. However, when two evenly matched bulls meet, a fierce battle can take place. Whereas the early fall "sparring" matches are mostly practice with a clattering of antlers, there's no mistaking a serious fight when the two combatants furiously lock antlers in an attempt to throw back their opponent amid dirt and vegetation flying through the air.

All this effort by the lustful bulls pays off the following spring when the cow ventures off on her own into dense cover to drop a single calf. The next few days are the most precarious for the newborn elk as they are vulnerable to coyotes, mountain lions, bears, and other predators. Within a few weeks the young calf and cow will rejoin the cow herds where they will find safety in numbers. Summer is a peaceful and tranquil time for the young calves; food is plentiful and they are under the watchful eye of their protective mothers. But come September a new rut begins and the belligerent bulls join the herds. For the calf, which has mostly lived a peaceful life only in the presence of cows, calves, and juveniles, the chaotic rut must be a confusing and upsetting period.

Elk Conservation

Prior to European settlement elk were widely distributed across North America and were found in myriad habitats, with the greatest densities probably being in the fertile savanna biome ranging from southern

Manitoba through Iowa and down to northern Arkansas. However, like all of the various deer species, elk abundance and distribution declined precipitously due to European settlement, unregulated hunting, and habitat destruction. By 1850 elk were extirpated from eastern North America. The decimation continued as the western states were settled. At their population nadir, only small numbers of elk survived and only in some of the most remote mountainous regions of the West. One of those remote areas was the Yellowstone ecosystem in northwest Wyoming. Once Yellowstone National Park was established in 1872 the elk population began to rebound because the animals were protected from hunting. Eventually, some Yellowstone elk were transferred to other park units, such as the newly established Wind Cave National Monument (now "Park") in the Black Hills of South Dakota. Elk are now recovered in much of the western United States and are found in many national parks. In fact, in some places the issue isn't too few elk, but rather, too many. For example, to keep the Yellowstone elk herd healthy and within the carrying capacity of the land the park reintroduced wolves. The elk herd there has now been restored to more natural levels and the vegetation is recovering.

Unfortunately, the recovery of elk in the eastern United States has not been as rapid. The subspecies that originally inhabited the region is now extinct; therefore, wildlife managers have resorted to transplanting the Rocky Mountain subspecies. Some of these transplanted elk have come from national park units, such as Theodore Roosevelt National Park in North Dakota. Fortunately, elk are adaptable and the reintroduced animals have generally been successful in their new habitats. One such successful site is the Buffalo National River in the Ozarks region in north-central Arkansas. The park is now regionally famous for its elk-viewing opportunities.

Parks with Elk

Buffalo National River, Arkansas

The crystal-clear Buffalo River is the lifeblood of the rugged Ozark Mountains of north-central Arkansas. In order to protect that priceless natural resource Congress established in 1972 the Buffalo National River,

Floating the Buffalo River. (Photo by Gary W. Vequist)

a unit of the National Park System and the first river in the country to receive such designation. This linear park now protects 135 miles of the 150-mile-long river. Just as significantly, the park protects 95,000 acres of Ozarks wilderness, including the forests and meadows essential for elk and other wildlife.

Buffalo National River is famous for its spectacular recreational boating and fishing—a key reason the park was established. The most prominent activities are those associated with the river: canoeing, kayaking, and fishing. One of the more scenic reaches of river is from the Carver Landing to the Mount Hersey Landing. This reach is somewhat lesser traveled, but still contains the dramatic cliffs, bluffs, and forested slopes the park is known for. Keep in mind that in the fall months some of the upper reaches of the river may have low water, which would make for

October–Elk of Buffalo River

Elk viewing at Boxely Valley. (Photo by Gary W. Vequist)

more portaging than canoeing. In addition to the river recreation there are also many upland activities such as hiking and horseback riding available. Also, large portions of the park are open to hunting (check with park staff for seasons and locations). A popular hiking trail that is in the nonhunted portion of the park is the Lost Valley Trail, which leads to the impressive Eden Falls, in the Boxely Valley area. A great one-two experience is to view elk in the early morning hours and then when the animals retire back to the trees hike the trail up to the falls (whether the falls are flowing is dependent on precipitation patterns).

Although the Buffalo National River was established primarily to protect the river and associated recreational activities, the reintroduced elk population now threatens to steal the show. Every fall as many as twenty thousand visitors travel to the park to view the elk, especially the magnificent bulls. The most popular viewing area is the Boxely Valley Historic District, where hunting is not allowed. The elk have learned they are safe in this area and hence are nonchalant about the traffic on the highway and the people at the viewing stations.

There is no single best place to see the elk because they are distributed throughout the valley. Early morning and dusk are the best times to see the elk because they are most active and visitation is generally less. Due to the popularity of elk viewing, the park has joined with the state of Arkansas to provide safe viewing platforms and other services for visitors. One important note; some of the land within the Boxely Valley Historic District is still in private ownership even though the area is within the national park boundary; respect the rights of the landowners as well as the elk by not venturing out into the fields.

For more tips on elk viewing and elk ecology visit the Elk Education Center in the town of Ponca (this quaint town is actually little more than a road junction). Arkansas Department of Game and Fish Commission employees staff the center. Another good education facility is the wildlife information center in the Hillary Jones Museum in Jasper, Arkansas. Park-operated visitor centers and information can be found at several ranger stations along the Buffalo River (the main park headquarters is in the town of Harrison, about 20 miles from the river).

MORE WILDLIFE IN THE OZARKS

Although elk have become the feature wildlife attraction in the park, there is a wide variety of other wildlife in the area because the region

Elk education center near the Buffalo National River. (Photo by Gary W. Vequist)

includes habitat features from the southwest, northeast, and southeastern United States. From the common (e.g., deer, turkey) to the unexpected (e.g., roadrunners, collared lizards) to the odd (e.g., armadillos, hellbenders), the park is a mix of all types of wildlife. Table 10 lists ten residents to look for at Buffalo National River:

Table 10. Animals of the Buffalo National River and Ozarks region

Elk	The Boxely Valley area and the entire park are becoming famous for their easy-to-see elk.
Turkey	Although they breed in the spring the males occasionally gobble in the fall, perhaps confused by the changing daylight.
Tree Squirrels	Both the larger and tawny fox squirrel and the all-gray gray squirrel can be found in the park.
Woodpecker	There are numerous species of woodpecker found in the park, with the most dramatic being the large pileated woodpecker.
Beaver	There are numerous dams in the Boxely Valley area, creating wetlands used by a diversity of other species.
Trumpeter Swan	Drive the Boxely Valley Road and one is almost certain to see a couple of these large, elegant white birds.
Opossum	North America's only marsupial; it is rare to see an opossum during the day.
Eastern Bluebird	One of the most colorful songbirds, they are found near the open fields where they hunt for insects.
Armadillo	This odd creature is mostly nocturnal. Sadly, one is most likely to see one where it was hit by a car.
Turkey Vulture	Circling turkey vultures are common as the park cliffs are ideal for roosting and for soaring on updrafts.

An unexpected surprise for many visitors to Buffalo National River is the presence of a small population of trumpeter swans. These elegant birds are the largest and still rarest waterfowl in the United States. At one time there were fewer than seventy trumpeter swans in the wild, mostly in remote rivers and lakes in and near Yellowstone National Park. Thanks to conservation efforts by a variety of agencies and organizations, and the support of the public, the species has recovered to the point that some birds have returned to their historic breeding areas in the Midwest. Several swans were moved from Iowa to Arkansas in an attempt to imprint the birds to use Arkansas for wintering habitat. Yet in an unexpected turn the birds decided to remain in the Buffalo River Valley in summer instead of migrating back to the Iowa nesting sites. At the old mill pond near Ponca, Arkansas, many elk watchers are lucky to see and hear the honking of these beautiful birds.

Other Parks with Elk

Elk can now be viewed in at least forty-six national park units scattered throughout the country. In fact, elk may now be one of the most widely distributed large mammals in national park units. From the Great Smoky Mountains National Park in the eastern United States to Point Reyes National Seashore along the Pacific Coast elk have made a dramatic comeback thanks in large part to national park units.

Yellowstone National Park, Wyoming

Yellowstone National Park is a sanctuary for the largest and probably most famous population of wild elk in the country, with about 30,000 animals calling the park home for at least part of the year. Nowadays, what makes the elk so famous isn't so much the elk per se, but rather their interaction with the reintroduced wolves. Visitors to Yellowstone National Park can often watch the struggle between predator and prey unfold right before their very eyes.

Grand Teton National Park, Wyoming

The Grand Teton National Park is known for its snow-capped mountains, tranquil ponds, and postcard scenery. Add to that several thousand elk and the visitor has an unforgettable wildlife-viewing experience. The largest wintering herds of elk in North America are in and near the park. The flat open range where the elk winter is known as Jackson Hole, and it includes a portion of the nearby National Elk Refuge. Elk viewing here is popular throughout the winter as thousands of elk move down from the mountains to spend the winter in the "hole." The Jackson Hole and Greater Yellowstone Visitor Center is a good place to learn more about elk ecology and management. For a unique elk-viewing experience visit in winter and ride on a horse-drawn sled that will take you among the wintering elk.

Rocky Mountain National Park, Colorado

Rocky Mountain National Park is the most famous, or infamous (depending on your point of view), park for elk viewing. This park has some of the most scenic elk viewing in the country, but also the most crowded. During the fall rut more than 500,000 people arrive to view elk. It can become so crowded that a shuttle bus is available on busy weekends so one doesn't have to fight the traffic jams to see elk. Rangers and scores of volunteers do their best to manage the crowds by directing traffic and assisting with parking. In addition to traffic management, the rangers ensure that elk watchers stay a safe distance away from the testosterone-stimulated bulls. Every October, the nearby town of Estes Park holds an Elk Festival to celebrate the animals. By most measures there are now too many elk in the park, causing destruction not only to the native vegetation within the park but also to the golf courses and lawns in Estes Park. As a result, the park has evaluated several options available to reduce the elk population, but unfortunately, the most ecologically effective method—reintroducing wolves—was not selected.

Niobrara National Scenic River, Nebraska; Theodore Roosevelt National Park, North Dakota; and Wind Cave National Park, South Dakota

The Great Plains includes three parks that have excellent elk-viewing opportunities. The Niobrara National Scenic River is well known for its remarkable mix of plant communities; deciduous and coniferous forests mingle with open prairies. The Scenic River includes the Fort Niobrara National Wildlife Refuge near the town of Valentine where visitors have a very high likelihood of viewing elk as they slowly drive the refuge's scenic wildlife drive. The same is true at Theodore Roosevelt and Wind Cave National Parks, where an early morning drive along the parks' roads most certainly includes passing by elk. The sight of grazing elk on the prairie at these three parks is similar to what Lewis and Clark witnessed two hundred years ago as they crossed the Great Plains. It's also a testament to the flexibility of elk (or what biologists would call *plasticity*) as they prosper in yet another habitat. Regarding Theodore Roosevelt National Park: we suggest contacting the park prior to visiting in late fall as park management may be conducting a culling operation to remove surplus elk.

Olympic National Park, Washington, and Redwood National Park, California

Olympic National Park supports the Roosevelt elk subspecies. This species of elk, named after Theodore Roosevelt, are the largest variety of elk in North America. They are most abundant in the Hoh Rain Forest area.

Point Reyes National Seashore, California

Farther south, but still along the Pacific Coast, can be found the rare tule elk in the maritime shrub lands and forests of Point Reyes National Seashore. Look for the elk in the small meadows and clearings in these parks.

Great Smoky Mountains National Park, Tennessee–North Carolina

Great Smoky Mountains National Park now hosts a small population of elk thanks to a reintroduction effort in 2001. The herd now numbers a few hundred animals with many residing in the Cataloochee area in the southeastern portion of the park.

9 ⌒ November

Beaver of Cuyahoga River Valley

Cuyahoga Valley National Park—located in northeastern Ohio just a half hour from the Cleveland metropolitan area and millions of people—is one of the newest parks in the National Park System. Surprisingly, even an "urban" park such as Cuyahoga Valley can conserve wildlife and provide quality wildlife-watching experiences. True, a visitor won't find wolves or grizzly bears, but one will find many other fascinating critters, including species deeply connected with America's heritage, like the American beaver. In some ways these new parks located near major metropolitan areas may be even more important than the remote wilderness parks in terms of conservation value, as they help to connect millions of citizens, including urban residents, with our natural resources. November is a great time to visit Cuyahoga Valley National Park and watch the beavers' handiwork (or should we say "toothy work") as they busily prepare for the coming winter.

What's Remarkable about Beavers?

The beaver is one of the few creatures that, like humans, can modify their environment to better meet their needs. Once a beaver finds a suitable site in a stream or small river it begins constructing a dam (how they determine a site "suitable" is unknown, but they seem to do a good job at it). The dam is constructed from branches the beaver has cut from the nearby

Viewers don't always need to see the animals to know they are around. Beavers leave as much or more sign than any other animal. (Photo by Gary W. Vequist)

uplands and mud it collects from the stream bottom or bank. The process and the logic that goes into building the dam is still somewhat of a mystery, but beavers typically start the dam by inserting some branches vertically into the streambed. This isn't an easy task; a beaver must jam the pointed end of the branch far enough into the substrate so that the current won't wash it away. The beaver then weaves horizontal branches between the vertical branches, all the time hoping that the vertical poles are fastened strongly enough to withstand the increasing water pressure on the dam. Mud and vegetation is then applied to strengthen the structure and to fill the holes. The entire construction may take months or even years. If the river or dam has a relatively steep grade the beaver may build a succession of dams, creating a stair-step series of ponds.

As testament to their engineering prowess, dams on small low-flow streams are often straight across, whereas those on large high-flow streams are often bowed upstream to better withstand the immense force of the water (think Hoover Dam). Some dams also have spillways to relieve the water pressure during high-flow periods. The longest known dam, in a remote area of Canada, was over one-half mile long and was actually discovered by satellite imagery. Once the dam is completed a pond starts to form, providing the beaver the ideal environment it needs for food, safety, and to raise a family. Of course, like any engineered structure the dam requires regular maintenance. It appears that beavers are stimulated to repair a dam by both the sound of running water and changes in current. In one ingenious experiment, beavers exposed to a loudspeaker broadcasting the sound of running water began piling up branches. However, beavers also find and readily plug underwater pipes with water flowing through, even though the pipes produce no sound (as far as we know). Whatever the stimuli, when a dam needs repair the entire beaver colony gets to work immediately.

Following the completion of the dam the next chore for the beaver is to construct a dome-shaped "lodge" out of more branches and mud. Within the cozy lodge the beaver will rest and raise a family. The structure is so solidly built that even bears cannot get to the occupants. The lodge's underwater entrance provides a safe exit for the beaver as well as reliable underwater access during the ice-covered winter months.

Yet the beaver's work is never done. The next task is for the beaver to

The old saying "busy as a beaver" is not without merit as the industrious animals are constantly repairing dams, building lodges, and stockpiling food, especially in the fall. (Photo by Daniel S. Licht)

create an underwater "cache" of green branches so that it has an accessible food supply during the ice-covered winter months. Some of the submerged branches may poke above the water's surface, which seems like a waste since they will be inaccessible once the pond freezes over; however, these branches poking through the ice will stop the blowing snow, thereby providing extra insulation above the cache. This means that the thickness of ice at the cache will be less, allowing the beaver access to more of the branches and perhaps even air pockets through which it can breathe.

As if that isn't enough work, beavers also excavate canals from the pond into the uplands. These canals provide a beaver with safe and easy access to the trees it fells for food and construction material. When all is said and done the remarkable beaver has created its own environment, home, grocery store, and roads.

Not only do beavers create their own habitat, they also create habitat for a wide variety of other animals. That is why beavers are considered a keystone species; their presence in the ecosystem benefits many other species. Native Americans called beavers the "sacred ones of the land" because they created habitat for many other animals. Even after the beavers abandon a pond their influence on the ecosystem is still felt as the pond changes over time to a marsh and then to a sedge meadow and then finally to a moist forest. All of these successional types support different and diverse communities of plants and animals.

Beaver Behavior

The American beaver has the distinction of being the largest rodent in North America (and second only to the capybara of South America), reaching 60 pounds in weight. On land beavers can be slow and plodding, but in the water they are fast and agile. Their specialized webbed feet efficiently propel them through water, and their flat tail makes a great rudder. They also have transparent eyelids to protect the eyes while underwater and long whiskers to help them feel their way when underwater visibility is poor. Their thick fur, protected with oil from the beaver's glands, keeps them warm even when the pond ices over in winter.

About the only time the beaver ventures onto dry land is to fell trees. Unlike the porcupine (the second largest rodent in North America and another bark gnawer), beavers can't climb trees, so to get to the palatable

The beaver dam changes a small stream into a pond, benefiting many species. (Photo by Gary W. Vequist)

twigs and buds they literally chew the tree down. If one is near a beaver pond at night and hears a tree crash in the forest it very likely could be the handiwork of a beaver. Once the tree is felled (aspen are preferred) the beaver will chew off the branches and drag them back to the pond where they will eat the bark and/or use the branches in the dam, lodge, or food cache.

Beavers typically live in extended family groups comprised of the adult pair, yearlings, and newborn kits. Most of their activity outside of the lodge occurs under the cover of darkness; however, they are often seen around sunset, and to a lesser degree, at sunrise (the fact that they are more commonly seen at sunset suggests that they can't wait to get started on the night's work). If a swimming beaver senses danger it will often slap its flat paddle-shaped tail on the water's surface, thereby creating a loud smack that warns other beavers in the colony that danger is near.

Beaver Conservation

Prior to European settlement there were millions of beavers distributed all across America from the Deep South to the Arctic tree line. Their dams, lodges, and felled trees were ubiquitous. Unfortunately for the beavers, the dams, lodges, and felled trees were like dollar signs to the early trappers. The beaver was, as much as any other animal, responsible for the opening of the frontier as trading routes, forts, and even communities were established for the purpose of trading beaver pelts.

As eastern beaver populations were decimated the fur trappers pushed west in search of new populations. In short time beavers were gone from much of the contiguous forty-eight states except for the more remote wildernesses and in places where they were protected, such as Yellowstone National Park. Eventually, the demand for beaver pelts subsided and game laws were enacted to protect the dwindling wildlife populations. Today, beavers have recolonized substantial portions of North America, including urban areas such as those in northern Ohio. After 150 years of absence, beavers have returned to the Cuyahoga Valley.

The return of beavers to the valley not only benefits other wildlife, it also benefits people in what scientists call "ecosystem services." For example, beaver dams slow river runoff thereby helping with flood control. The dams also retain polluted river water, with many of the pollutants eventually being filtered out within the pond. And during dry periods the beaver ponds serve as water reservoirs that replenish groundwater supplies. These services can be worth millions of dollars. Consider that the Cuyahoga River that flows through the valley was once so polluted it actually caught fire (a tragedy so infamous it helped inspire passage of the Clean Water Act). The beaver, along with concerned citizens and better laws, can help protect water quality in the valley.

Parks with Beavers

Cuyahoga Valley National Park, Ohio

Once upon a time the thought of a large national park just 30 minutes from Cleveland and Akron, Ohio, would have been considered a fantasy, but in 2000 it became a reality with the establishment of the Cuyahoga Valley National Park (prior to that the site was designated a "recreation area"). Although surrounded by urban and suburban areas, the park seems worlds away in terms of the sights, sounds, and smells. The park is

Beaver nibbling at a cache of branches collected for surviving the winter. (Photo by Daniel S. Licht)

an oasis of forests, fields, and wetlands. The Cuyahoga River (the "crooked river" as Native Americans called it) meanders through the park for 22 miles and is the unifying natural resource within the park.

Being a young park, and one established in the heavily developed Cuyahoga Valley, the restoration of natural resources at the park is a work in progress. In many cases the restoration and preservation of natural resources needs to take into account the rich cultural farming history of the site. For example, the park maintains many former farmlands as part of a pastoral landscape. In other places the park is restoring the habitat to pre-Columbian conditions. One such example is the 70-acre Beaver Marsh, now one of the healthiest wetlands in the park. Prior to the federal government's acquisition of the site, it was home to an auto salvage yard. Once it was acquired volunteers removed the debris and cleaned up the site. And then beavers moved in and finished the job by building dams to hold water in the marsh. Where there was once garbage there is now a vibrant beaver marsh and healthy ecosystem. The site symbolizes the environmental recovery of the Cuyahoga River Valley.

Cuyahoga Valley National Park is located within a half-hour drive of millions of people, so it's not surprising that the park caters to outdoor recreationists of all types. For example, the park has numerous biking trails, with one of the more popular trailheads starting at the Peninsula Depot Visitor Center. The site just happens to be next to a small wetland with a beaver lodge. A good half-day bike adventure meanders along the towpath north to the Brecksville Depot, while a daylong bike ride contin-ues farther to the Canal Visitor Center Depot.

Of course one need not be a bicyclist to take the Cuyahoga Valley Scenic Railroad. One can ride the train and enjoy the scenery while also experiencing a bit of history. The train passes several wetlands where bea-vers may be present. Traveling by train may be viewed as old-fashioned, but it is actually an environmentally friendly way to view wildlife. The Cuyahoga Valley Scenic Railroad also provides an alternative transporta-tion from Akron and Cleveland to the park (weekends only in November).

For a unique and educational outdoor activity consider helping the park on a wildlife survey. The park has an active volunteer citizen-scientist group whose members participate in long-term monitoring of butterflies, amphibians, and bird populations. Such an experience not only helps park managers, it also gives the public insight and experience in wildlife conservation. Contact the park for more information.

The Beaver Marsh, as the name implies, is one of the best places to look for beavers at the park. Disembark at the Indigo Train Depot for a short walk to the start of the Beaver Marsh Trail (also known as the Ira Road Trailhead). An elevated boardwalk provides an excellent viewing platform of the beaver pond. There are several good places nearby to relax and observe the wildlife. Remember, dusk is by far the best time to observe not only beavers but also a whole host of other wildlife. During

The Cuyahoga Valley Scenic Railroad provides a unique way to see the nature and history of Cuyahoga National Park. (Photo by Gary W. Vequist)

daylight hours it's unlikely the beavers will be active, but one can look for other signs of beaver activity, such as fallen trees, chiseled branches, lodges, canals, and dams.

Wildlife sightings at a beaver pond vary from season to season. November is one of the best times to see beavers as they are busy preparing for winter; however, the diversity of wildlife is greater in spring through early fall because many insects, amphibians, and migratory birds are more active. With those seasonal changes in mind, try to discover the following ten animals (table 11):

Table 11. Wetland animals found at Cuyahoga National Park

Beaver	Be at the pond at dawn or dusk and you greatly increase your odds of finding this important animal.
Wood Duck	The colorful drake wood duck almost seems out of place in the gray November light.
Muskrat	The muskrat is often misidentified as a small beaver. They too make lodges, but not out of sticks.
River Otter	This charming species has returned to Ohio and can now be seen at the Beaver Marsh and elsewhere in the park.
Indiana Bat	Bats love wetlands because of the insect prey; however, this endangered bat is done flying come November.
Great Blue Heron	Sit patiently for a half hour or so and you should witness a blue heron striking for fish, frogs, and other prey.
Red-Winged Blackbird	The iconic wetland songbird and the voice of the wetland during the spring and summer months.
Painted Turtle	The common turtle seemingly found in every wetland in North America.
Raccoon	Abundant everywhere there's water, you may only see their tracks as they're mostly nocturnal.
Mink	Everyone has heard of a mink coat, but few people realize the animal can be found in their backyard.

Too much wildlife?

Yes, it's happening throughout North America, including in many of our national parks. Deer and elk are two of the biggest culprits. In fact, overabundant ungulates may be the single biggest issue facing wildlife managers in national parks. When deer and elk numbers exceed what the land can support, the vegetation suffers. Look at the trees about 5 feet off the ground and you can often see a "browse line" where there are few leaves and branches below that height. The degradation can in turn affect all of the other animals that depend on a healthy ecosystem. Outside of national parks, hunting helps to keep deer and elk numbers in check, but hunting is prohibited and problematic in most national park units. Hunting also has shortcomings; hunters don't typically take the weak animals in the way that natural processes would. The irony of the problem of too much wildlife (e.g., deer) is that it is the result of too few wildlife in the form of large predators (e.g., wolves, mountain lions, and bears).

An experienced wildlife observer knows that the wildlife-watching experience is greatly enhanced if one looks for signs as well as the actual animals. For many animals the chances of actually seeing the critter may be slim as they are rare, nocturnal, or intolerant of people; however, their signs may be quite evident. Not surprisingly, children are usually the first to find animal tracks in the mud along the edge of a beaver pond or to notice chewing on trees. A field guide can help identify what animal made the tracks, left the droppings, or chewed the tree. Fortunately, there are numerous field guides written to help wildlife watchers identify tracks and other signs.

It's hard to believe that the white-tailed deer was once almost gone from Ohio and much of the eastern United States. Nowadays, almost everyone has seen a white-tailed deer, if not in a national park then per-

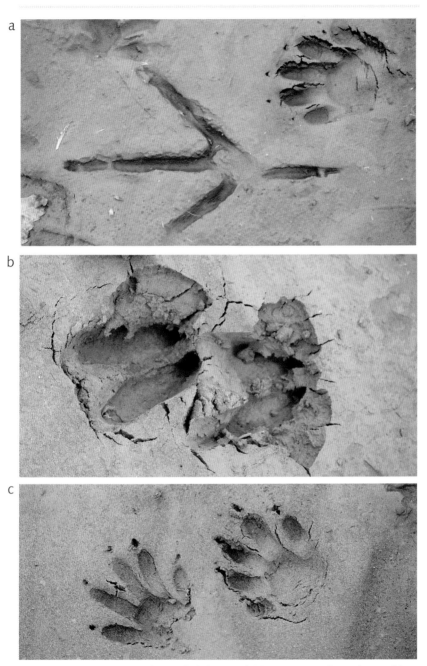

(a) Great blue heron, (b) white-tailed deer, and (c) raccoon tracks in the mud by a beaver pond. (Photos by Gary W. Vequist)

haps in a state park or even in a backyard as the species is incredibly adaptable. In fact, white-tailed deer are so adaptable and prolific that in the absence of hunting and natural predators (e.g., wolves) they can quickly overpopulate an area. Unfortunately, this is the case in many national park units where deer populations are viewed as being larger than what the habitat can support, thereby threatening the health of the plant communities and, indirectly, other wildlife populations. The overabundance of deer and other ungulates presents a management dilemma for park managers as they try to protect and conserve the health of park ecosystems.

Unfortunately, all of the potential options for reducing deer populations, ranging from the reintroduction of predators to using sharpshooters or hunters to cull surplus animals to using reproductive control are problematic. Ultimately, the decision as to how to proceed is made on a park-by-park basis, typically with significant input from local communities and concerned citizens as well as the best available science.

White-tailed deer are so abundant in many parks they threaten to impact the vegetation and the health of the ecosystem. (Photo by Gary W. Vequist)

The beaver "tail slap" is a warning to other beavers that danger is near. (Photo by Daniel S. Licht)

More Parks with Beavers

In pre-Columbian times beavers were found throughout North America; soon after European settlement they were absent from much of North America outside of Canada and Alaska. They are now once again abundant in most of their former range. They are so widespread that beavers can be found in 164 park units.

Grand Teton National Park, Wyoming

Grand Teton National Park provides arguably the most scenic landscape in which to view the American beaver. This park is the site of a historic fur trader rendezvous. Seeing as how fur trapping once eliminated beavers from large parts of North America, it is ironic and fitting that one of the best places to now see beavers is near where the trappers used to get together. That the site is in the shadow of the scenic Grand Teton Mountains enhances the wildlife observer's experience. Beaver activity can change from year to year, but a generally reliable place to see beavers in the park is along the Moose-Wilson Road.

Acadia National Park, Maine

Acadia National Park, with its deep forests and abundant wetlands, provides numerous opportunities to look for beavers and other wildlife. Beavers were once extirpated from the park and perhaps all of Maine, so they were reintroduced to the park in 1921. A study found that beavers have increased the amount of wetlands in the park by 89 percent over the past fifty years. Many of the freshwater birds (e.g., herons and ducks) that benefit from the reintroduction of the beavers can be seen at Beaver Dam Pond. For a quieter wildlife experience hike the historic carriage trails to the numerous backcountry lakes and wetlands.

Saint Croix National Scenic Riverway, Wisconsin

The Saint Croix National Scenic Riverway protects the 252-mile-long Saint Croix River system and surrounding uplands. The park provides plenty of opportunities for a wild and picturesque canoe adventure through prime beaver habitat. The headwaters of the river were historically a portage site for French fur trappers plying the interior of the United States for beaver pelts. Stop at the park visitor center in St. Croix Falls, Wisconsin, to find out which beaver ponds in the park are active.

Voyageurs National Park, Minnesota

Voyageurs National Park may have more beavers (two to three per square mile) than any other national park unit. The park abuts the Canadian border, right smack in the middle of the beaver country traveled by the French Voyageurs. Although beavers are abundant in this vast park, to see them one is best served by taking a boat. Fortunately, there are several places one can rent boats, including houseboats for taking overnight trips deep into the park wilderness. Or, for a more authentic north woods experience, take a canoe and paddle deep into the wilderness to pitch a tent. Soon one will hear nothing but water dripping off a canoe paddle and the occasional loon singing its haunting call. Keep in mind that the park is in northern Minnesota so it's better to visit early in the fall, as much of the park is ice-covered by November.

Isle Royale National Park, Michigan

Although relatively more difficult to get to because it requires a visitor to take a ferry, floatplane, or large seaworthy boat, Isle Royale National Park in Lake Superior is also an excellent place to see beavers. The island park has thousands of lakes and wetlands of all sizes, many occupied by beavers. In addition to an abundant beaver population, the park is also home to moose and wolves. Moose are yet another beneficiary of beavers as they often venture out into the beaver-made ponds in the summer to escape biting flies and to feed on aquatic plants. Isle Royale is truly a wilderness park and should be on every outdoor enthusiast's "bucket list"; however, one can't get to the park in November because there are no commercial boats operating due to the inclement weather. Summer is the most popular time; however, September is by far the most scenic and the most pleasant as most of the biting insects are gone.

Winter

Bison in winter at Yellowstone National Park. (Photo by Gary W. Vequist)

There is always something fascinating to discover in America's national parks. This holds true even in winter. Undeniably, in many northern parks the harsh winters and icy roads can test the wildlife observers' dedication, just as winter tests the perseverance of the mammals and birds that brave the inclement weather. And in a northern winter there are often fewer animals to see because many birds have migrated to faraway places while many mammals, reptiles, and amphibians sleep away the winter months in their hibernacula.

Yet there are many great and unexpected wildlife-viewing opportunities in winter. For example, some animals do not hibernate or migrate and in many ways are much more active and interesting than they are in the lazy summer months. Also, some species are actually easier to spot in the winter as they gather in large congregations and in very predictable areas. Another plus to wildlife viewing in winter is that in many parks one may have the site all to oneself, a far contrast from the crowds and traffic of summer. In winter a park visitor can experience a sense of peace and solitude that is difficult to find in the other seasons. So, wildlife viewing in winter is not only rewarding, it can actually be more rewarding than in the other seasons, especially if one knows when and where to look.

In the following three sections we highlight three species representing three different classes of the animal kingdom (reptiles, mammals, and birds). All wildlife observers hold the American alligator, gray whale, and bald eagle in high esteem.

In south Florida many animals, like alligators, do not migrate or hibernate, making it possible to view them year-round. Winter is actually the best time to view alligators; the temperatures are tolerable, the bugs less buggy, and migrants from up north have joined the resident wildlife.

On the Pacific Coast, in Northern California, whale watchers travel out in January to the scenic Point Reyes coastline to search the ocean surface for migrating gray whales. The shore-hugging migration of the gray whale makes them relatively easy to spot. For wildlife observers it's almost as if a parade is passing by, albeit with widely spaced participants. The spouting mists from their blowholes are as timeless as the waters they swim in.

Winter—a little extra work, but it's worth it

Face it! Some animals are just not easy to see in the wild because they're secretive, nocturnal, or scarce. Even experienced outdoorsmen can go their entire lives without seeing a mountain lion, lynx, or mink. Yet in the winter you can see the next best thing, their tracks. In fact, by following their tracks through the snow, as they travel, hunt, scavenge, and interact with members of other species, you can actually learn more about the animal than you would if you caught a glimpse of it fleeing through the brush. Head outdoors after a fresh snowfall and you will have a great wildlife adventure.

Far away from either coast, in snowy Minnesota, birdwatchers clothed in down jackets and mittens come from throughout the Midwest to see the large gatherings of bald eagles congregated near the unfrozen sections of the upper Mississippi River. These majestic birds swoop over open water snatching whatever fish, waterfowl, or other prey they can. They need to eat fast as other eagles may move in to steal the catch. By late winter, adult eagles are beginning their acrobatic courtship displays in preparation for the nesting season just around the corner. So in reality, winter is far from a dead period; it is actually a great season to visit a national park and watch wildlife.

10 ⌒ December

American Alligators of the Everglades

Winter in the Everglades sounds like an oxymoron, but there is indeed a noticeable winter season. Instead of snow and subfreezing temperatures, relative dryness and pleasant temperatures characterize the region (versus the steamy heat of summer). Winter in the Everglades is also characterized by increased biodiversity as northern migrants join the resident wildlife. Scores of wading birds and waterfowl seem to occupy every waterhole. And lurking in the water and along the shores are the ubiquitous alligators, waiting for a chance to lunge at unsuspecting prey. Far from being a quiet season, December in the Everglades can be action-packed.

What's Remarkable about Alligators?

Almost all aspects of the American alligator are fascinating, from their bone-crunching jaws to their hundreds of millions of years of evolution to their unique anatomical and physiological features. One particularly odd alligator characteristic that is both remarkable and cause for conservation concern is the fact that the temperature of the nest almost solely determines the sex of newborn alligators. If the nest temperature is 86 degrees or lower all of the young will be female, whereas if the nest temperature is 93 degrees or higher all of the young will be male (nests in the midrange can produce both sexes). The primary determinant of the temperature seems to be the material the nest is built of. Nests constructed of

The recovery of the American alligator ranks as one of the country's greatest conservation stories. (Photos by Gary W. Vequist)

leaves tend to be hotter than those constructed of moist marsh vegetation. Over their hundreds of millions of years of evolution alligators have somehow managed to find a nice balance, so there's always enough males and females to keep the species going. But what happens under climate change? Could we end up having all male young, or will the alligators adjust by using moister and cooler material to construct their nests?

Alligator Ecology

The American alligator is a survivor. For about 200 million years they've persevered, while other reptiles, including the mighty dinosaurs, disappeared from the face of the earth. The alligator has been rightfully referred to as a living fossil, and seeing one is perhaps the closest any of us will ever get to a time machine.

Of course, part of what makes alligators so fascinating is their teeth, their jaws, and the way they patiently wait for prey. A favored hunting tactic is to float like a water-soaked log with only eyes and nostrils exposed above the surface. In this position they can wait motionless for hours until prey comes close enough for an attack. Science recently discovered that alligators have a sixth sense located in nodules on the rim of

The American alligator can grow up to 19 feet long and weigh a half a ton, making it a top predator wherever it is found. (Photo by Gary W. Vequist)

their jaw that serve as water-motion detectors. If the sensory organs detect prey within striking distance the alligator lunges and snaps in an effort to catch the unsuspecting prey. This hunting method is especially useful in catching fish, which often constitute a large portion of their diet.

In addition to fish, alligators will eat almost anything, including other alligators in a cannibalistic battle to the death. Even turtles with their hard shells are on the menu, although it's not uncommon to see a gator bite off more than they can crunch when they take on a particularly large turtle. Wildlife watchers can sometimes see a gator holding a large turtle in its mouth for hours—as if trying to decide what to do next. However, in most cases all one sees of an alligator predatory attack is a flurry of splashing, a few swift chomps, and then the alligator throwing its head up in the air to swallow its prey. With larger prey it may take longer as the alligator, or alligators, have to tear, crunch, and pull the prey apart using the infamous "death roll."

Much like the wolves in Yellowstone, alligators are at the top of the food chain, and their presence has a ripple effect throughout the ecosystem. For example, a significant prey item of alligators is the prehistoric-looking spotted gar (a fish). When alligators are abundant few spotted gar survive long enough to reach 2 feet in length. When there are fewer of these large gar there are likely to be more small fish. This in turn means there's more small fish for wading birds such as herons and egrets. So somewhat ironically, alligators actually benefit herons and egrets, although they're not above taking one of the birds when the opportunity presents itself. For this and other reasons the alligator is often considered a keystone species.

In addition to controlling prey numbers, alligators indirectly affect other species. For example, female alligators construct enormous piles of mud and plant debris in which to lay their sixty or so eggs. Snakes and turtles often take advantage of these structures by depositing their own eggs in the mounds.

The female alligator guards the nest for two months, ferociously protecting the eggs from potential threats, including other alligators and even people. This trait makes alligators somewhat unique among reptiles in that they have a strong maternal instinct—they care for their young. The hatched alligators will stay with their mother for up to two years and are frequently seen clinging to her head and back. More than one person has been given a good scare by getting too close to young alligators, not realizing that an angry mother is nearby.

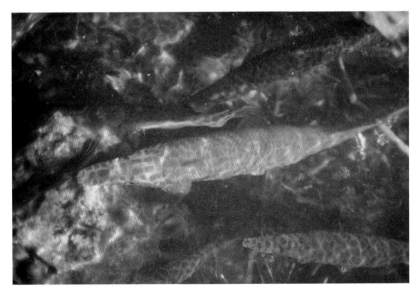

Spotted gar; a favorite prey of alligators. (Photo by Gary W. Vequist)

Alligator Conservation

Once widely hunted for their skin, the American alligator almost became extinct. Thanks to the Endangered Species Act—and the alligator's ability to lay up to sixty eggs per nest—they have recovered (they are still technically listed as threatened, but only because they are similar in appearance to the endangered American crocodile, and many hunters can't tell the species apart). Today, these semiaquatic reptiles are common across the Florida Everglades and throughout much of their historic range in the southeastern United States. Alligators again fulfill their ecological role as apex predator, mound builder, waterhole excavator, and system regulator. Yet challenges remain to protect alligators and their habitat. Nowhere is this truer than in the delicate Florida Everglades ecosystem.

There are several threats to alligators in the Everglades. Using water from the Everglades for agricultural and municipal needs threatens to destroy the ecosystem. Without water the Everglades would cease to exist. Compounding the problem is the fact that the water that does reach the glades is often polluted from pesticides, fertilizers, and municipal runoff. But out of problems sometimes arise solutions, and this may be the case with the Everglades. For example, in recent years a series of federal-state

Alligator munching on a turtle. In this case the alligator bit off more than it can chew. (Photo by Sandy Vequist)

partnerships have enabled better management of water resources in the state in order to restore and protect the priceless Everglades.

Unfortunately, new threats keep popping up. For example, the recent invasion of nonnative Burmese pythons into the Everglades threatens to wreak havoc on Everglades' wildlife. Even alligators may be at risk because the snakes take alligator eggs and young. Yet perhaps the largest threat to the glades ecosystem is still on the horizon. When humans first arrived in southern Florida (12,000 or so years ago) the glades may have been twice as large as they are today. Over time, sea levels rose, turning the lower glades into a marine habitat. Today, most of what remains of the Everglades is less than 3 feet above sea level. Global warming and the associated melting ice caps and rising sea levels could inundate much of the remaining glades, the stronghold of the American alligator.

Parks with Alligators

Everglades National Park, Florida

Nowadays, alligators can be seen throughout much of the southeastern United States. In fact, in some areas they are now considered a pest. So, going to the Everglades to see alligators may seem unnecessary. Yet the Everglades are an exceptional place that has had an exceptional role in the conservation and recovery of the species. At the time of the alligator's population collapse, when their very existence seemed in doubt, it was primarily in Everglades National Park that the alligator managed to hang on. This is one of the priceless values of America's national parks: they are the last sanctuaries for many of our imperiled species. And that's why alligators are synonymous with Everglades National Park.

The Everglades is barely higher in elevation than the adjacent sea. In its simplest description it is a vast expanse of shallow, slow-flowing fresh water through a prairie of sawgrass, that is, a "river of grass." The water moves at the rate of only one-quarter mile per day, taking a full year to cross the glades and reach the mangrove coasts. Just 6 inches deep, but 70 miles wide, the glades are like no other wetland ecosystem on earth. In places the open expanse of sawgrass disappears over the horizon and the "river of grass" and sky converge into one scenic landscape.

A blue heron waiting for an unsuspecting fish, frog, or other prey. (Photo by Gordon Dietzman)

Not surprisingly, Congress was slow to realize the value and potential of the Everglades as a national park unit. Prior to the park being established, most potential parks were evaluated based on their geologic features and scenic grandeur (e.g., mountains, waterfalls, coasts). It's not a stretch to say that the Everglades, while serene and vast, do not meet everyone's idea of scenic grandeur. Yet the Everglades are a stunningly beautiful landscape in their own unique way. And they are biologically rich, so much so that the site has been designated an International Biosphere Reserve.

Everglades National Park is not an easy park to access. There are really only two vehicle entrances to this vast 1.5-million-acre park; the Main Park Road from the east (Miami) side and the Shark Valley Loop Road from the north. The Main Park Road goes all the way to the Flamingo Visitor Center area, with many noteworthy places to stop at along the way. Two miles past the park entrance is the Royal Palm Visitor Contact Station, the starting point for the Anhinga Nature Trail. This half-mile boardwalk traverses the Taylor Slough, penetrating deep into a wet natural world. It is one of the best trails in the park to take to see wildlife, especially birds and alligators. The animals are, of course, wild but have become accustomed to seeing a steady stream of people on the boardwalk. This trail may have more wildlife per distance than any other nature trail in North America.

Continue along the main park road as it traverses the "river of grass" and other habitats for about 40 miles until it reaches its saltwater terminus at Flamingo. Along the way are several excellent pull-offs for viewing wildlife and stretching one's legs, like the West Lake Trail. Although Flamingo is a hub of human activity one will still see plenty of fascinating wildlife, including brown pelicans trying to steal fish from fishermen and ospreys eating fish in the live oak branches just above one's head. At Flamingo visitors can rent bikes, canoes, kayaks, and other gear and can charter fishing boats or sightseeing cruises.

Perhaps the most exhilarating and iconic Everglades recreational experience is an airboat ride. With their flat bottoms and powerful fans these

A purple gallinule. The large feet allow it to walk on lily pads in search of prey. (Photo by Daniel S. Licht)

boats easily glide over the shallow water and grassy wetland vegetation. Commercial operators can be found all along the Tamiami Trail, the highway that runs east–west adjacent to the park's northern boundary. Many of the operations are owned and run by indigenous Miccosukee Indians, adding to the visitor's experience.

One of our favorite places to view wildlife is the Shark Valley area, specifically, the 15-mile loop road (there are no sharks there; the site gets its name from the fact that water flows from Lake Okeechobee into the Shark River and then into the heart of the Everglades). The loop road leads to the Shark Valley Observation Tower, providing one of the best views of the glade ecosystem. Cars are not permitted on the loop road; however, visitors can ride an open-air tram. This tram frequently stops to allow riders to view wildlife, especially alligators sunning on the right-of-way. The more adventurous can take a bicycle (rentals are available), stopping at their discretion to observe the flocks of ibises, herons, wood storks, gallinules, and other showy birds. We strongly recommend taking the trail in the early morning hours for several reasons: 1) wildlife is most active, 2) the parking lot and trail are less congested, and 3) the lighting is at its best for taking photographs.

WILDLIFE AROUND AN EVERGLADES WETLANDS

At first glance parts of the Everglades might seem like a monotonous "sea of grass" sparsely populated by wildlife. But there are biological hotspots within the apparent uniformity. Find open water and the visitor will find one of nature's more diverse habitats. Listed below (table 12) are just a few of the many animals found hunting, feeding, resting, nesting, fighting, or simply sleeping undisturbed.

The Everglades are famous for their biological diversity, especially for their birds. Every prime fishing spot seems to be occupied by scores of wading birds (e.g., ibises, egrets, herons), either frozen in place or slowly stalking the shallows ready to strike out to grasp an unsuspecting fish. This diversity and abundance makes the Everglades one of the most popular birding areas in the United States, attracting both experienced and novice birders. Because of the diversity of bird life a bird field guide is essential to differentiate the species, age classes, and plumages (birds wintering in southern Florida may have different plumage than they

Table 12. Charismatic animals of the Deep South and Everglades National Park

Alligator	They're in almost every wetland; just remember, they rarely move. So look closely at that bump in the water as it may be an alligator.
Florida Gar	Like the alligator, this fish is a survivor from the age of dinosaurs. Polarizing glasses will help you see them in the water.
Wood Stork	The only stork to breed in North America, these ungainly birds may have as many as 25 large stick nests in a single tree.
Roseate Spoonbill	Hard to mistake this glamorous pink bird for anything else. They feed by swinging their bill back and forth in the water, filtering out prey.
Snail Kite	This hawklike bird feeds almost exclusively on snails; the snail population depends on a healthy Everglades hydrology.
Purple Gallinule	A metallic-purple bird walking across lily pads. If you forget how to pronounce the name, just remember, "gal I knew."
Manatee	The supposed "mermaid" of lore, they are an endangered species. Collisions with boats remain a high concern for the species.
American Crocodile	In the Everglades the alligator is at the southern end of its range, whereas the crocodile is at the northernmost end of its range.
White-Tailed Deer	Bergmann's rule says that southern animals are smaller, allowing better heat dissipation. The tiny Everglades deer are an example.
Florida Panther	Consider this the sighting of a lifetime. A secretive, rare, and endangered cat. If you see one, tell a park ranger.

have during the summer months up north). For many birders the Everglades provides numerous opportunities to add new species to their life lists, like the gaudy purple gallinule. Some species, such as the snail kite and limpkin, are endemic to Florida. Hard-to-find birds like the roseate spoonbill and the wood stork draw birdwatchers from all over the world.

What is the most bizarre bird in the Everglades? It is hard to choose with so many species, many of which are uniquely adapted to the ecosystem. However, for many birders a species that stands out is the anhinga. The locals call the anhinga the "snakebird" because of its long, thin neck. This slender bird swims with only its head and neck above the water surface, somewhat like a submarine with only the periscope above water. When it sees a fish the bird sinks underwater and spears the fish with its

Anhinga drying its wings. (Photo by Daniel S. Licht)

pointed beak. Once a fish is caught the anhinga faces a new dilemma: how to dislodge the impaled fish from its bill. One solution commonly deployed is to flick the fish up into the air and then open wide to swallow the fish head first. Another curious trait of the primitive bird is that it lacks an oil gland to repel water. Hence it has to climb up on a bush or other object to spread its wings and dry off. Watching waterlogged birds attempting to climb up a tree can be rather comical. Once the wings are dry the anhinga can again fly off, or if it chooses, flop back into the water and do some more spearfishing.

Other Parks with Alligators

Fifteen National Park Service units report alligators as present in the park. Three parks—Big Cypress National Preserve, Canaveral National Seashore, and Everglades National Park—report them as being abundant.

Big Cypress National Preserve, Florida

This national preserve's namesake features are the six-hundred-year-old bald cypress trees, yet for many visitors the most captivating attraction is the countless alligators. Located on the eastern border of Everglades National Park, the preserve may be an even better place to see alligators; the animals are numerous along the Tamiami Trail (an unfitting name for a high-speed two-lane highway) and at viewing platforms at Williams Roadside Park and at the Oasis Visitor Center. Everglades City is one of the gateway communities for the park; from there one can take guided boat tours past mangrove bays and into the coast of "10,000 Islands."

Jean Lafitte National Historic Park and Preserve, Louisiana

Jean Lafitte National Historic Park and Preserve supports wildlife of all kinds at the 23,000-acre Barataria Preserve unit in Louisiana, located an

The Shark Valley Trail at Everglades National Park is one of the best bike trails in the country: flat, paved, and with little traffic and lots of wildlife. (Photo by Daniel S. Licht)

hour away from New Orleans. The slow-moving bayous of the Mississippi River Delta nourish this cypress swamp. Look for alligators in the darkened water of the Spanish moss–draped bayous. The preserve has observation decks and bird blinds nestled among marsh vegetation, providing concealment while viewing birdlife. There are also walking trails and boardwalks for venturing into the alligator hideouts. Deep in the swamp visitors may feel as if they've gone back hundreds of years. However, if a visitor simply cannot do without modern technology he or she can use a cell phone for an audio tour of what is seen along the trail. The more adventurous may rent kayaks and canoes for a backcountry expedition through this gator-rich park.

11 ✍ January

Gray Whales of Point Reyes

Think a person needs a large boat and/or lots of money to see whales? Not at all. Whale watching can be done from shore—if one knows where to go. One of the best places to see whales from shore is Point Reyes National Seashore, an hour's drive north of San Francisco, California. In fact, studies have shown that 94 percent of the migrating gray whales along the Pacific Coast swim within a mile of the park. So not only can one see whales, one can do so without getting seasick. Southbound gray whales begin to show up off Point Reyes in late November, with their numbers peaking around mid-January. The northbound migration peaks in mid-March, with the cows and their calves passing through as late as April and early May.

What's Remarkable about Gray Whales?

The gray whale is one of the nine "great whales," a group that includes the largest animals ever to grace the planet (the blue whale is usually given the title of largest). The gray whale, although about one-third the size of the blue whale, still weighs an astonishing 70,000 pounds and can reach 45 feet in length (longer than a city bus). How do whales get so large? The answer is genetics, long lives, and lots and lots of food. To acquire that food, gray whales gulp in enormous quantities of water and bottom sediment and then filter out small crustaceans with their specialized comb-like filters called baleen. Compared to other baleen whales that feed in the

Gray whale looking at the observer. (Photo by Craig Hayslip)

water column, the gray whale has specialized shorter baleen that is better suited for straining out the bottom-dwelling marine invertebrates it prefers. Another unique characteristic of gray whales is their peculiar way of swimming sideways while stirring up sediments on the muddy sea floor. It's possible that this strange behavior, combined with the whale's sensory organs, helps them better find and consume food buried in the muck.

Whale Migration
Animals do not migrate just for the heck of it. There has to be a reason. For the gray whale it comes down to the fact that the Arctic Ocean is rich in food during the summer, but the warm waters of the equatorial Pacific are a much better place to rear young and spend the winter. Hence, every year the gray whale logs about 12,000 miles on this round-trip migration, perhaps the longest migration of any mammal. In fact, the gray whale spends about one-third of its life in migration.

The cold Arctic waters are rich in nutrients and oxygen. Under the twenty-four hours of summer sunlight phytoplankton flourishes. These tiny drifting plants are in turn consumed by masses of zooplankton (small drifting animals). In Arctic waters these tiny marine organisms can occur in densities hundreds of times greater than in tropical waters. The biomass of these tiny creatures becomes so great that, ironically, some of the largest creatures on earth actually survive on them. During the summer feeding season a gray whale in the Arctic can consume over a ton of zooplankton and other food a day. This enormous intake quickly builds up fat reserves (i.e., blubber), which is critical because once the whales return to the warm and relatively barren waters near the Baja Peninsula they rarely eat.

Gray whale mating occurs during the southbound migration from November to February; however, the gestation period is so long (about thirteen months) that the calves will not be born until the following winter after females return to the warm shallow lagoons of the Baja Peninsula. It is there that a cow gives birth to a single calf, which she will aggressively protect from sharks and orcas. As spring approaches the cows and their newborn calves will be the last to leave the warm-water nurseries for the North Pacific feeding grounds.

The classic image of a gray whale fluke. (Photo by Craig Hayslip)

Migrating whales stay submerged for three to four minutes before resurfacing to exhale through their two "blow holes." The sighting of a whale above the surface may only last for a few breathtaking seconds, adding to the mysterious aura of an animal we still understand little about. It's a sight that has inspired and fascinated people since they first inhabited the Pacific Coast thousands of years ago.

Whale Conservation

The first whalers of European descent arrived on the Pacific Coast about two centuries ago. They initially targeted the relatively slow right whales (named "right whales" by early whalers because they were the "right" whales to hunt), but the whalers quickly shifted to gray whales when they realized that gray whales migrated close to shore and on a predictable timetable. These traits were almost the demise of the gray whale; in fact, the Atlantic Ocean population was hunted to extinction as early as the eighteenth century. On the Pacific Coast, whaling stations sprung up around the 1850s. Not only were gray whales taken during the biennial migrations, they were harvested at both their warm-water calving lagoons and at their Arctic feeding grounds. Oftentimes, entire families of gray whales were unsparingly taken (whalers sometimes called gray whales "devil fish" because the cows fought valiantly to protect their young). By 1900 virtually the entire Pacific Coast gray whale population had been slaughtered, with perhaps fewer than three hundred animals surviving. At such a low density it was no longer profitable to hunt gray whales, so whalers turned their harpoons to other species, such as sperm whales. Reprieve eventually came to the remaining whale stocks when numbers were so low the whaling industry collapsed, a victim of its own unregulated zeal. Economists and ecologists sometimes refer to this oft-repeated cycle of overharvesting as a "tragedy of the commons," whereby everybody takes as much as they can from the same shared resource with little regard to conservation or long-term sustainability. Eventually, everybody suffers. Although limited whaling for some species still continues to this day, international prohibitions and regulations have helped recover many species.

Thanks to these conservation laws the current population of about 22,000 gray whales may be close to what the ocean can support, although

The ocean, the crashing of the surf, and the sighting of a whale have a timeless mystical quality that has been passed on for generations. (Photo by Gary W. Vequist)

Want to protect wildlife, see great places, and meet interesting people?

If so, consider becoming a "wildlife docent." A docent is a volunteer who works at a park, specifically one that teaches and guides the public. Docents do things like patrol beaches, greet visitors, and operate observation decks (under the guidance of park staff, of course). Their primary job is to promote awareness and protection of wildlife by interacting with the public. The most important skill is to be a good communicator. Point Reyes National Seashore recruits docents specializing in elephant seals, snowy plovers, gray whales, tule elk, and other wildlife. The park also recruits volunteers for wildlife surveys and other tasks (these may be under more strenuous conditions). Contact your favorite park for volunteer-in-parks (VIP) program opportunities.

some argue that historic levels may have reached 100,000 animals. Regardless, the species has recovered to the point that the federal government no longer lists it as endangered. The gray whale recovery is undoubtedly one of the more remarkable and uplifting stories in wildlife conservation. Unfortunately, the same is not true for all whale species. Consider that the blue whale population is believed to be less than 1 percent of its historic population size; as a result, the species remains on the list of endangered species.

Parks with Gray Whales

Point Reyes National Seashore, California

Although only an hour north of San Francisco, Point Reyes' rocky shoreline, with its unobstructed views of sky and sea, has the feel of untouched wilderness. The Point Reyes landmass juts 10 miles out into the Pacific Ocean. This scenic peninsula is filled with peaceful lagoons, rocky shorelines, and grassy uplands, all the result of the tectonic uplift that created it. In fact, the eastern park boundary is smack on top of the famous San Andreas Fault. From the peninsula's promontories the Pacific Ocean sinks westward beyond the viewer's vision. Winter is the best time to visit the park because the sky is often clear (compared to the foggy summer days). The clear view once prompted the old-time mariners to shout "All clear on the western Pacific!"

In terms of recreational activities, the park has over 150 miles of hiking trails through a wide diversity of habitats (a unique trail is the Earthquake Trail, which explains and highlights the San Andreas Fault geology). Trails are also available for bikers and horseback riders, although there are restrictions. There are also numerous beaches to explore, but once again, check with park staff as some may be closed or have restricted access to protect elephant seals, breeding seabirds, or other marine life

Today, chances for seeing whales between December and April in Northern California are so much a "sure thing" that some tour-boat excursions guarantee it. Yet no one needs a boat to see these leviathans. Each year whale-watching enthusiasts gather at numerous strategic locations

The walk to the Point Reyes lighthouse. (Photo by Gary W. Vequist)

along the peninsula to view the migrating whales, reliving the maritime sailor's cry of "thar she blows." Although several whale species can be spotted from the Point Reyes' headlands, the gray whale is by far the most common.

When heading to the park to view whales one's first stop should be the Bear Valley Visitor Center to pick up the park newsletter, the "Pacific Gray Whale." If arriving on a weekend or holiday try to get there early and get a shuttle bus schedule. Starting in 1998 the park began operating a shuttle bus service during the peak whale-watching period of January to mid-April. The shuttle bus system has successfully eliminated traffic congestion problems that once backed cars up for miles waiting for a parking space near the Point Reyes Lighthouse. Although the shuttle bus service is effective and well run, we suggest visiting the park during weekdays when private vehicles are allowed and there is less congestion at the more popular whale-watching sites.

Once at the lighthouse parking area, there is a paved trail that summits at the lighthouse visitor center—two hundred and seventy steps above the lighthouse itself. The visitor center is staffed by national park rangers and volunteers who are available to answer questions. It is also an excellent vantage point from which to spot whales.

The more adventurous can trek along a 1-mile dirt path to the Chimney Rock Overlook. This grassy-rounded ridgetop is surrounded on three sides by precipitous cliffs (off-trail terrain is treacherous, so stay on the trail for safety). The view from this promontory is awe-inspiring and well worth the hike. On clear winter days these coastal headlands are a perfect location to watch gray whales navigate around the knife-edged sea stacks.

January is the peak whale-watching month, but the migration continues into April. In April it can be more difficult to spot migrating whales; however, it is sometimes worth the effort as newborn calves accompany their mothers. The young whales roll and spin in frivolous play, whereas the adults are all businesslike as they efficiently swim northward. Another reason for an April visit to the park is that the bluffs and points come alive with wildflowers, adding to the nature experience.

Harbor seal resting on beach. (Photo by Gary W. Vequist)

Shorelines are great places for bird watching. This whimbrel is relatively easy to identify, but some of the other shorebirds can test one's identification skills. (Photo by Gary W. Vequist)

WILDLIFE AT POINT REYES SEASHORE

The stunningly beautiful California coastline competes for one's attention while one scans the vast ocean for migrating whales. Of course, the splendor of the landscape doesn't detract from the wildlife-viewing experience, but rather enhances it. Coastlines are great places to see a diversity of wildlife as the two dramatically different ecosystems of sea and land come together. Perhaps there is no better example of that than the elephant and harbor seals that feed out in the ocean waters, but haul out on the park beaches to rest. During a winter day bring binoculars and try to find the following marine animals (table 13):

Table 13. Ten marine species found at Point Reyes National Seashore

Gray Whale	Best sites to see one are the headlands such as Chimney Rock, Sea Lion Overlook, and the Point Reyes Lighthouse.
Harbor Seal	An inquisitive seal that will follow boats; look for them off Point Reyes beaches, Bolinas Lagoon, and in Drakes Estero.
Harbor Porpoise	A small porpoise that stays close to shore, it is commonly spotted by whale watchers.
Northern Elephant Seal	In 1910 there may have been fewer than 1,000 in existence; today there are about 2,000 just in the park.
Great White Shark	A top marine predator, they prey on elephant seals and other prey off the Point Reyes Headlands.
Surf Scoter	A 2007 oil spill in San Francisco may be partially responsible for the 50–70 percent decline over the past forty years.
Common Murre	It only comes ashore to nest. The bird uses its wings for underwater propulsion and dives as deep as 600 feet.
Snowy Plover	Listed as threatened under the ESA, this perky shorebird should only be viewed from afar.
Sea Otter	Look for these charming animals bobbing offshore. Oil spills continue to be a significant danger to this threatened species.
Brown Pelican	Almost extirpated due to DDT; now that the pesticide is banned the species has made a remarkable comeback.

Point Reyes National Seashore is also famous for its bird watching, with hundreds of interesting birds to observe. The seashore claims the greatest bird diversity of any national park in the United States, with 490 recorded species (45 percent of all the bird species in North America). Many of the documented species are transitory migrants, meaning that the species composition and abundance at the park changes by season, and often within a matter of just a few days.

Perhaps the most charismatic, and yet, unattractive species at Point Reyes National Seashore is the elephant seal. Breeding pairs of these behemoths only recently showed up at Chimney Rock after being absent from the park for over 150 years. This massive seal is easy to recognize during breeding season because the males (known as bulls) use their large proboscis (snout) to emit a raucous trumpetlike call signaling their dominance and fitness to mate. Adult males sometimes battle in a titanic kind of neck wrestling and chest butting. Their migration compares somewhat

The elephant seal's odd proboscis is used to emit its loud mating calls. (Photo by Gary W. Vequist)

to the gray whale in that they inhabit the park in the winter and spend the summers in the food-rich feeding grounds of the North Pacific. Although seemingly slow and clumsy on land, elephant seals are amazing swimmers. They can dive to depths of 2,000 feet or greater (the deepest documented dive was 5,000 feet). These impressive depths would be instantly fatal to humans, but elephant seals have specialized traits that help them survive the high-pressure deep dives.

RESPONSIBLE MARINE MAMMAL VIEWING

Watching marine mammals in their natural environment can be a positive way to promote conservation and respect for marine animals. However, irresponsible human behavior can disturb wild animals, destroy important habitat, and even result in injury to animals and people. To promote responsible and sustainable wildlife watching, Point Reyes National Seashore has developed educational materials, viewing guides, and regulations. Practicing good ethics allows visitors to get the most out of their experience while safeguarding marine mammals for future generations.

Shorelines are great places for viewing wildlife as two ecosystems come together. (Photo by Gary W. Vequist)

Other Parks with Whales

Eight parks, all in California or Alaska, report gray whales as being present. Keep in mind that the presence and abundance of whales varies by season.

Golden Gate National Recreation Area, California

This national recreation area's boundary encompasses two dramatically different worlds: the urban southern end of the Golden Gate Bridge, including the Presidio of San Francisco, and the relatively natural Marin headlands at the north end of the bridge. The Marin Headlands area has spectacular wildlife viewing that rivals that at nearby Point Reyes National Seashore; the biggest difference is that the Headlands include

Urban wildlife watching at Pier 39 in San Francisco. From there you can take whale-watching charters. (Photo by Gary W. Vequist)

stunning views of the Golden Gate Bridge as well. One highly recommended hike takes a paved trail from the Marin Headlands Visitor Center about half a mile down a ridge, with San Francisco Bay on the left and the Pacific Ocean on the right. The trail will take one through an old tunnel to the Point Bonita Lighthouse for a unique view of the bay. Another worthwhile stop is the nearby Marine Mammal Center where one can tour the exhibits and view rescued seals and sea lions being rehabilitated back to health.

On a clear day the Farallon Islands can be seen 27 miles to the west of the Golden Gate National Recreation Area. The US Fish and Wildlife Service manages these islands as the Farallon National Wildlife Refuge. They are noted for the largest seabird breeding colonies in the United States; the migrating gray, humpback, blue, and fin whales that pass nearby; the large colonies of California sea lions and elephant seals on the shores; and the great white sharks that visit the waters around the islands every September to November to feed on the young seals and sea lions. In the winter months whale-watching excursions depart daily from San Francisco's wharfs to view the marine animals around the islands.

Channel Islands National Park, California

Channel Islands National Park is sometimes referred to as "The Galapagos of the North." Near the southern end of the California Coast this island park protects a diversity of habitats supporting over one hundred endemic species specially adapted for survival in the island's harsh environment. These species have evolved in isolation much like the species Darwin observed on the Galapagos Islands. The park has more marine mammals (whales, porpoises, seals, and sea lions) than any similar-sized location in the United States. One of the reasons the waters surrounding the park are so plentiful with life is that they are enriched by an upwelling of nutrients from 6,000 feet below the ocean's surface (a submarine canyon as deep as Arizona's Grand Canyon). The islands are also ringed by submerged kelp forests that attract an array of marine mammals, fish, and seabirds. One-third of the entire world population of northern elephant seals (50,000) belly-up on Channel Island beaches during winter months. The Santa Barbara Channel, which separates the islands from the mainland, is a premier place for viewing whales. Twenty species of whales travel past the islands each year, with boat tours leaving throughout the year from Santa Barbara and Ventura harbors. The biggest surprise is the

Whale watching from the coastal cliffs of California. (Photo by Gary W. Vequist)

January–Gray Whales of Point Reyes   189

The "spy hop" of a humpback whale. (Photo by Paul Brown)

recent observation of around two hundred blue whales off the Channel Islands. Blue whales were drastically reduced during the first half of the twentieth century (360,000 were harvested between 1910 and 1965). Their population is slowly rebuilding, yet it's estimated that only 1,700 animals now occur in the coastal waters of California.

Cabrillo National Monument, California

Cabrillo National Monument is another great place to see whales in January. The Point Lomas bluffs offer commanding views of the Pacific Ocean and present-day San Diego. The park commemorates the site where Juan Rodríguez Cabrillo, an Iberian conquistador, explorer, and seafarer landed on the Pacific Coast in 1542 (believed to be the first time that a European set foot on the west coast of North America). It later was the site of a whaling station. The Old Point Loma Lighthouse (built in 1854) is an excellent spot from which to watch whales. California sea lions and harbor seals can also be found in the waters surrounding the 160-acre park.

Acadia National Park, Maine

Acadia National Park is noted for its humpback whale watching. Whale-watching boats depart daily from Bar Harbor, a quaint vacation town on Mount Desert Island. In addition to seeing whales on these charter boats one may also see puffins, porpoises, dolphins, and a variety of other marine life. It's ironic that many of the old whaling seaports along the Atlantic Coast (like Salem and New Bedford), now serve as departure points for the whale-watching tours that bring in millions of dollars to local economies. The popularity of whale watching is a testament to how far society has changed in its perception of these magnificent creatures. Regrettably, gray whales are no longer found in the Atlantic Ocean.

12 ⟋⟋ February

Bald Eagles on the Mississippi River

Are we seriously recommending wildlife watching in Minnesota in the dead of winter? Well, "you betcha." True, Minnesota in February is cold and, for much of the state, seemingly lifeless. But an exception is the unfrozen reaches of the Upper Mississippi River where thousands of bald eagles congregate, attracted by the hundreds of thousands of ducks, geese, and other waterfowl. And much of this fantastic wildlife viewing is close to the millions of people of the Minneapolis–St. Paul metropolitan area. The National Park Service manages much of this amazing wildlife-watching area in partnership with numerous other agencies and organizations. The story of the bald eagle, and the Mississippi National River and Recreation Area, is a fitting conclusion to our twelve-month story of wildlife watching in national parks.

What's Remarkable about Bald Eagles?

The story of the bald eagle is a microcosm of the country's wildlife history. Our Founding Fathers were impressed by the power and majesty of the bird, so much so they made the bald eagle our national symbol (contrary to popular lore, there is no strong evidence that Ben Franklin seriously preferred the turkey as a national symbol). Yet despite this admiration, some perceived the bald eagle as standing in the way of progress, so we waged war on the bird by shooting, trapping, poisoning, and

America's national bird and a fitting symbol of wildlife conservation in America. Once on the verge of extinction, bald eagles have recovered thanks to public support and conservation laws. (Photo by Daniel S. Licht)

persecuting it. Inevitably, the eagle soon disappeared from large parts of the country.

Then, with the eagle on the brink of extirpation in the lower forty-eight states, a societal shift occurred. Society became concerned about the plight of the eagle and many of our other disappearing wildlife species. As a result, we passed laws to protect the eagle and other imperiled species, and their populations soon recovered. Perhaps more importantly, the plight of the eagle and our other wildlife species demonstrated how inextricably linked we are to our environment. If the eagle was dying, then the environment—our environment—was dying. Conversely, if the eagle population was healthy, then our environment was healthy. The recovery of the eagle is a remarkable success story, but what's even more remarkable is the larger story of how far people have come in terms of our relationship with our wildlife heritage and the environment we share with wild animals.

An adult bald eagle. Immature eagles are mostly brown and lack the striking white head and tail feathers. (Photo by Gordon Dietzman)

Eagle Wintering Habitat

Until about eighty years ago there were few if any bald eagles that wintered in the Upper Mississippi River Valley in Minnesota, Wisconsin, and Iowa. In most winters the relatively slow-moving Mississippi froze solid. However, the construction of a series of locks and dams changed the flow patterns of the water. Immediately below the man-made structures the water flowed faster and was often warmer. These water releases kept open portions of the river even during the coldest periods. In short time waterfowl took advantage of the open water by "short-stopping" their historic southward migrations. Eagles soon followed suit, attracted by the abundant prey. Whether this altering of natural patterns is a good thing or not depends on one's point of view. However, what isn't debatable is that these changes have created a great opportunity to watch bald eagles, waterfowl, and other wildlife on the Upper Mississippi River throughout the winter months.

Southbound bald eagles begin congregating along the Upper Mississippi River in November, although the timing varies from year to year depending on weather conditions up north. An early cold snap up north means the eagles show up earlier, a late onset of winter means the opposite. The eagle's arrival has less to do with the bird's cold tolerance than it does with the availability of open water and prey resources. Even when temperatures dip below zero eagles can be seen perched on the frozen branches along the Upper Mississippi River, patiently watching and waiting for a meal. The dense layers of feathers (they have about seven thousand warmth-trapping feathers), combined with a diet of high-nutrient fish and waterfowl, is all the eagle needs to get through the harsh Minnesota winter.

In winter eagles congregate near open water where fish, ducks, and other prey are abundant. (Photo by Daniel S. Licht)

The majestic cottonwood and oak trees lining the Upper Mississippi River provide ideal vantage points from which eagles can scan patches of open water in search of food. Sometimes a half a dozen or more birds will be perched on strategically positioned trees. Trees near the dam tailraces are especially attractive as fish are sometimes killed or dazed as they pass through the dam's outlets. And with thousands of waterfowl using the open water it's just a matter of time before an eagle spots one that is sick, weak, injured, or otherwise vulnerable. And even if the eagle is not the first one to the prey, they are not above a little thievery as they try to steal the catch from other animals, including other eagles. It's not uncommon to see an eagle swoop down to pluck a fish out of the water and then see several other eagles quickly mob their kin in an attempt to steal the prize.

Eagle Conservation

The sharply hooked bill, menacing talons, and intense stare of the bald eagle give it a fierce look. That's just one of the reasons the eagle is on the Great Seal of the United States. Unfortunately, our relationship with our national symbol has not always been a good one. Bald eagles and other raptors were victims of the misguided practice of predator control conducted in the early part of the twentieth century. By 1940, when Congress passed the Bald and Golden Eagle Protection Act, their numbers had declined significantly, and there were only about four hundred nesting pairs in the United States (Alaska not yet being a state). That law prohibited the shooting of eagles, but eagle numbers did not immediately rebound. Two decades later it was discovered that the birds were once again declining, this time due to a silent killer—pesticide poisoning. The bald eagle, being at the top of the food chain, would consume large quantities of fish, waterfowl, and other prey species that had residues of the pesticide DDT in their bodies. The eagles would "bio-accumulate" the poisons in their bodies, which led to sterility or, if the eggs did fertilize, abnormally thin eggshells that were often crushed under the weight of the incubating birds.

At first, only a few underfunded scientists, often struggling in anonymity, knew about the problem. Then an ecologist by the name of Rachel Carson put pen to paper and wrote *Silent Spring*. The landmark book eloquently and dramatically identified pesticides as a killer of wild-

The Mississippi National River and Recreation Area is located in the Minneapolis–St. Paul area. The site provides wildlife-viewing opportunities for millions of people. (Photo by Gary W. Vequist)

life, perhaps at unfathomable scales, and maybe even leading to the extinction of some species, including the bald eagle. More profoundly, she made the case that if all of these birds were declining due to pesticide poisoning it might be only a matter of time before humans would be poisoned as well. In other words, the birds were our "canary in the coal mine," warning us that our environment was becoming inhospitable. As a result, DDT was banned in the United States. Nowadays all pesticides must undergo rigorous testing before they can be approved and, once approved, there are strict limits on their application. This is good for eagles as well as for people.

Today, the bald eagle has made a triumphant comeback, to the point that there are over ten thousand breeding pairs across America; the species is off the endangered species list. One of the largest gatherings of bald eagles can be found along the banks of the Upper Mississippi River in Minnesota, Wisconsin, Iowa, and Illinois. In the 1960s Rachel Carson organized winter eagle surveys along the Upper Mississippi River that turned up a mere fifty-nine birds; today, over 2,500 bald eagles have been counted along this 300-mile stretch of the "Mighty Miss." The presence of these eagles not only inspires and thrills the wildlife watcher, the birds have also benefited local communities because thousands of tourists come each winter from far and wide to observe and marvel at the amazing spectacle of such large numbers of our national symbol.

Parks with Bald Eagles

Mississippi National River and Recreation Area, Minnesota
Much of the 72-mile-long Mississippi National River and Recreation Area lies within the cities of Minneapolis and St. Paul, Minnesota, and their nearby suburbs. But don't be fooled by the location. Despite being located in a metropolitan area of three million residents, this river corridor is home to an amazing diversity of wildlife and countless opportunities to view them.

The Mississippi National River and Recreation Area is a new breed of National Park Service unit in that the federal government actually owns very little land within the "park boundary" (often referred to as the park's *administrative* boundary). In fact, one won't see many boundary signs nor will one find the park on most maps. Established in 1988, this park accomplishes its mission of conserving wildlife and providing wildlife-watching opportunities by partnering with local landowners and with other federal, state, and local agencies. Many visitors may not even be aware they are recreating within a National Park Service unit, but the agency is there, often working behind the scenes to ensure that the site protects the wildlife therein for present and future generations. For example, a couple of the things the park does is monitor water quality in the river and take blood samples from eagle hatchlings to test for the presence of contaminants.

As the name implies, the Mississippi National River and Recreation Area was established in large part for outdoor recreation, and the park lives up to that mission. In fact, there are so many outdoor activities in and near the park they are too numerous to even start listing here. Therefore, we encourage readers to check out the park's web page as it lists a variety of activities in a variety of locations and in all seasons. Another good starting point is the Science Museum of Minnesota, a nationally renowned museum located in downtown St. Paul overlooking the Mississippi River. The museum has

Hawk migration

Roughly 40 percent of the nation's migratory birds pass through the Mississippi Flyway every spring and fall. On their southward journey many birds of prey (hawks, falcons, eagles, and the like) reach Lake Superior's north shore. Preferring not to cross the vast expanse of water, they follow the shoreline. Once they reach the lake's southern tip near Duluth, Minnesota, they— with barely a flap of a wing—soar on the updrafts above the 600-foot escarpment known as Hawk Ridge. This congregation of soaring hawks, eagles, and falcons is known worldwide by bird watchers. Hawk Ridge Nature Reserve in Duluth is an exceptional location to view this migration spectacle, or drive along Sky Ridge Road to the Hartley Nature Center above the city and get a bird's-eye view of the raptors. As they head southward the birds will pass through the Saint Croix National Scenic Riverway, the Mississippi National River and Recreation Area, and Effigy Mounds National Monument.

dozens of galleries and exhibits on the history and ecology of the Mississippi River. Within the museum is a Mississippi National River and Recreation Area Visitor Center staffed by National Park Service rangers.

The Mississippi National River and Recreation Area and its partners have done an amazing job of preserving natural riverine habitats within the highly developed river valley. In winter, bald eagles and waterfowl are the prime wildlife-viewing attraction. And the site is equally famous for the large numbers of wintering waterfowl. In fact, the waterfowl populations in the park in winter rival what one will find on many National Wildlife Refuges, most of which were specifically established for waterfowl conservation.

So bundle up and head out to watch wildlife in a Minnesota's winter wonderland. And if it's an exceptionally cold morning and there are second thoughts about venturing out, keep in mind that such days are

Waterfowl viewing is spectacular in the winter when open water congregates large numbers of birds. (Photo by Daniel S. Licht)

actually the best days for eagle watching as the portions of open water shrink even more, meaning the birds are even more congregated (once again, whether this is good ecologically is another matter).

Wintering bald eagles can be found anywhere within the park administrative boundary wherever there is open water. That even includes sites within the Twin Cities metropolitan area. However, locations can vary from year to year depending in part on weather conditions; we recommend contacting the park for current information. A few places are especially reliable year after year. One such place is the 215-acre Hastings River Flats Park near the town of Hastings, specifically, at Lock and Dam #2. Scores of eagles use this site each winter.

Another great site is just south of the Mississippi National River and Recreation Area at the Colville City Park in Red Wing, Minnesota. In early winter over one hundred thousand common mergansers, loons, and grebes raft together in this part of the river. Even in February the number of waterfowl is in the tens of thousands. The sheer number of swimming birds tends to keep the water from freezing. And where there's lots of waterfowl there will be lots of eagles. Even farther south along the "Great River Road" that parallels the west bank of the river is Wabasha, one of Minnesota's oldest towns. Wintering bald eagles can be seen from several vantage points in and near the town. The town is also home of the National Eagle Center, a nationally recognized eagle recovery center. This nonprofit facility is also a great source of eagle information.

MORE WILDLIFE IN THE EAGLE'S WINTER HABITAT

One of the joys of watching bald eagles in their winter habitat is that there is other hardy wildlife to watch as well, with many of the species congregated at the open water. Most notable is the large flocks of mallards, goldeneyes, scaup, coot, geese, and other waterfowl. Look closely and it's possible to see a dozen or more species—all in the same flock. There is also wildlife in the riparian forests and uplands, although one will have to look harder to find these resilient winter residents (table 14). While at the Mississippi National River and Recreation Area look for these ten hardy wildlife species:

Table 14. Riparian wildlife found along the Upper Mississippi River in winter

Bald Eagle	Look for the majestic birds soaring overhead, perched in tall trees, or standing on the river ice.
Pileated Woodpecker	Listen for the loud rapping of this majestic crow-sized woodpecker on the large trees in the riparian forests.
Crow	Crows keep an eye on eagles in hopes of getting a few tidbits when the eagle is done feeding.
River Otter	Perhaps more than any other species, otters seem to enjoy winter as they slide and play in the snow.
Mink	Everyone seems to know what a mink coat is, but few people realize that they are common along the Mississippi River.
Waterfowl	The Mississippi River in the winter is a waterfowl watcher's paradise with all kinds of ducks, geese, and other water birds.
White-Tailed Deer	The fact that this deer is now "common" makes it no less admirable as it survives through the tough Minnesota winter.
Red Fox	The bright red fur of this fox stands in stark contrast to the white snow and gray trees.
Great-Horned Owl	February may seem like the dead of winter, but amazingly, great-horned owls are starting to lay eggs already.
Black-Capped Chickadee	The black-capped chickadee flutters among the trees of the riverbank calling a wishful "spring-come-soon."

In April the river ice begins to thaw and the Mississippi River Valley comes alive. The narrow valley is a major thoroughfare for migrating birds, with all kinds of species passing through. Although many of the birds migrate at night, others pass through during daylight hours. Large aeries of hawks are some of the more noticeable migrants. The bluffs along the river make for a relatively easy migration for the hawks as they soar on the updrafts. They use the steep bluffs much like pilots use a jet stream (e.g., to save on fuel). It makes for some great raptor watching.

Other Parks with Bald Eagles

It's a testament to how far the United States has come in conserving its wildlife resources that 212 park units now report bald eagles as being present in the park, at least for a portion of the year. That's also a testament to the rich diversity of habitats national park units support.

Effigy Mounds National Monument, Iowa

Effigy Mounds National Monument is downstream from the Mississippi National River and Recreation Area. The park protects ancient Indian burial grounds overlooking the Mississippi River far below. This reach of the river is one of the most scenic with its towering bluffs and large expanse of riparian forests. Once winter subsides about two-dozen pairs of eagles stay to nest in the vicinity of the park. During their courtship displays the excited eagles will dive at each other, sometimes locking talons and tumbling precariously through the air. It looks like they're out of control, but it is all part of the pair-bonding ritual that has been going on for millennia. Once the birds are convinced they're meant for each other they will select or build a nest in a large tree, often near the river. In April the chicks hatch, and around June they are ready to leave the nest. The following February they will add to the large concentration of eagles looking for prey on the Upper Mississippi River.

Missouri National Recreational River, Nebraska–South Dakota

This national park unit is similar to the Mississippi National River and Recreation Area in that the National Park Service actually owns very little land. To conserve wildlife within the administrative boundary the agency partners with private landowners and other federal, state, and local entities. Located on the Nebraska and South Dakota border, this site includes two free-flowing reaches of the Missouri River, each below large hydroelectric dams. The best wintertime locations to watch bald eagles are immediately downstream of the dams. From the Lewis and Clark Visitor Center at the Gavins Point Dam (near the town of Yankton) one can peer down at eagles perched on tall cottonwood trees along the river's edge. Another great location is downstream of Fort Randall Dam. Spend an hour or so by the dam's tailrace and one will almost certainly see eagles swooping down to pick up fish from the water or testing the fitness of the thousands of waterfowl on the river. This park unit commemorates the epic journey Lewis and Clark took as they explored the vast American wilderness and its wildlife. It's only fitting that the symbol of our country can once again be found along this reach of the Missouri River.

Upper Delaware Scenic and Recreational River, New York–Pennsylvania

Upper Delaware Scenic and Recreational River is a spectacular whitewater river on the border of New York and Pennsylvania. The site gets extremely cold in the winter, but fast-flowing rapids keep portions of the river from freezing, thereby attracting bald eagles. This scenic park supports the largest population of over-wintering bald eagles in the Northeast, with more than one hundred birds using the area during January-February. The nonprofit Eagle Institute works closely with the park on eagle conservation. One of the things the institute does is provide volunteers at eagle-viewing sites to assist visitors.

Olympic National Park, Washington

Bald eagles are common in several national parks in the Pacific Northwest, including Olympic National Park, where they may be found along the coastline or farther inland feeding on salmon and other fish in the rivers and lakes.

A youngster watching eagles and other wildlife from inside a science museum along the Mississippi River. (Photo by Gary W. Vequist)

North Cascades National Park, Washington
The winter gathering of eagles on the Skagit River gravel bars near North Cascades National Park coincides with the seasonal arrival of one of their favorite foods, salmon. The river flows through the Bald Eagle Natural Area (managed by several agencies and landowners) where spawned-out salmon carcasses attract eagles.

Lake Roosevelt National Recreation Area, Washington
Also look for bald eagles and ospreys (known as "fish hawks") at Lake Roosevelt National Recreation Area. Ospreys are much more efficient fishers than eagles, so the eagles often turn to stealing the osprey's catch. Not very majestic behavior on the part of our national symbol, but it is all part of nature's way.

Final Observations

According to the US Fish and Wildlife Service, eighty-seven million Americans enjoy some form of wildlife-related recreation. Those Americans spend more than $122 billion annually in wildlife-related activities (e.g., binoculars, lodging, birdseed, etc.). These numbers do not include the large number of foreign visitors who come to the United States to visit Yellowstone and our other national parks in hopes of seeing our charismatic wildlife heritage. It is indisputable that wildlife watching is significant to the country, socially as well as economically.

We hope this book contributes in some small way to helping people get out and view wildlife. We especially urge parents to take their children on a wildlife safari, even if it's just down the road to a small national, state, or county park. We believe that today's wildlife watcher becomes tomorrow's conservationist. Such a cycle can and should become self-perpetuating. That would be good news for our wildlife, our parks, and our country.

As this book shows, no matter the season and the location, there are countless opportunities to watch wildlife in its natural habitat. To increase your success of seeing the critters, spend some time learning about the animals, their behavior, and their habitat. One can then more accurately predict when and where to see them and what they will be doing. If available time for wildlife watching is limited, as it is for most of us, such preparation will allow one to plan for the best days to be afield. Of course, there is no bad time for viewing wildlife, so if there is a spare day grab the binoculars and camera and head out to the field and enjoy wildlife.

Wildlife viewing is a flexible activity in that it can be done alone or with others, and both approaches are fulfilling. Alone, a viewer can go at his or her own pace, where one wants, and for as long as one wants. However, there is also something special about sharing a wildlife-watching experience with others. One way to enhance a wildlife viewing experience is to take a child. True, young children can be noisy and may scare some animals away, which can be frustrating, but children can also open one's eyes to things that might otherwise pass by. Many adults need to relearn how to look at and enjoy the natural world. Sometimes we are only looking for the large predators and other charismatic species we see on television. In contrast, young children have an innate fascination with all living things, big and small. They are fascinated by that banana slug that adults often pass right by. Tracks in the mud can lead to dozens of questions. A simple puddle is waiting for discovery and exploration. In many ways, children have the desire, perception, pace, and curiosity for truly discovering nature. They just need an adult to take them. So why wait?

Hints for Viewing Wildlife

1. Do your homework. When planning your wildlife-viewing trip do your homework. Research your target species, their behaviors, and the best viewing locations and times. Nowadays you can get much of the information you need from the Internet. But for the best up-to-the-minute information contact people in the know. Park staff should be your first contact if heading to a park unit (for other public lands contact the appropriate offices; for nonpublic lands contact your state wildlife agency).

2. Have the right gear. Your outdoor experience will be much more pleasant and will last longer if you're properly dressed, have water, food, sunscreen, insect repellant, and other quality gear such as binoculars or spotting scopes (don't skimp on the optics; quality binoculars start at around $200). And don't forget your field guides. Even experienced naturalists still occasionally need help. There are field guides for everything from butterflies to marine mammals.

Go slow and be patient and you will observe more wildlife. (Photos by Gary W. Vequist)

3. Bring an expert (or at least someone more experienced than you). You can enjoy wildlife watching all by yourself, but if you're a novice and you want to become a really good wildlife watcher in a short period of time there is no better way than learning from someone with more experience and knowledge than you have. Remember the first time you sat down in front of a computer; it was overwhelming and you didn't know where to start. Wildlife watching can be the same way. If you have someone to help you then you will be less likely to get frustrated and quit, and if you keep at it eventually you will become the expert.

4. Go slow and be patient. Wildlife observing requires people to slow down and take their time. Experienced wildlife observers, including professional wildlife filmmakers and photographers, know that you often have to spend many hours outdoors to witness that special event. We've literally spent days waiting for that predation event, but in the end it was worth it. True, going fast may actually increase the number of animals you see, but quality observations occur when you go slowly.

5. Use all your senses. When thinking of wildlife watching you automatically think of using your eyes (after all, it's called wildlife "watching"), but experienced outdoors people know your other senses are just as important, especially your ears. Bird "watchers" have known this for years. In fact, many bird surveys are done primarily by sound; that is, the observer never actually sees the bird, but records its presence based on the call. And don't forget your other senses. Yes, on occasion we've even smelled wildlife before we saw or heard it.

6. View from afar. Wildlife viewing should be done from a distance whenever possible. This is for your own safety, but there's another reason as well. If you're viewing from a distance the animal will tolerate your presence and go about living its life. If you're patient you may see something truly spectacular or interesting, such as a predation event or animals mating. Use a spotting scope or binoculars

The observer effect

Scientists have long known of the "observer effect." The observer effect essentially states that *anyone who observes a system becomes part of that system and thereby affects the very system he or she is observing.* This applies to wildlife viewing. Anyone who watches wildlife becomes part of what is happening. Sometimes that is obvious, as when the animal flees because of the observer. Other times it can be subtler, for example, maybe the animal was going to head your direction, but decides to leisurely veer off in another direction due to your presence. You may not realize the effect you had because the animal seemed unalarmed. Another example, perhaps the area where wildlife viewers congregate would be an ideal site for a den, nest, or foraging area, but it's not used because of the presence of people. As we've stated throughout this book, parks are for both people and wildlife, yet this interaction between people and wildlife is a constant challenge for park managers as they try to keep people safe and animals behaving naturally. When the people, the "observers," affect the system to the point that the wildlife is not behaving naturally then managers must intervene. In some cases, such as with bears that have learned to associate people with food, this can have fatal consequences because the park must remove the "problem" animal. Yet that animal only became a problem because of the observers. As one park biologist stated, "the easiest way to manage bears is to close the park to people." That of course will not, and should not, happen; the best solution is for wildlife viewers to practice good ethics so they have a minimal effect on the wildlife they are observing.

and view from a hidden observation point (car or viewing platform) and be patient. You will then have some of your best wildlife-viewing experiences.

7. Be out at sunrise and sunset. Where to go? and what season to go? depends on your target species, so there is no right answer regarding those questions. But with very few exceptions, there is a best time of the day to view wildlife, and that is at sunrise or sunset. A large majority of the more charismatic species is active at these times of the day. In fact, many wildlife species are considered "crepuscular" (meaning active at sunrise and sunset). Sunrise is an especially good time to be out in a national park, as you won't have to face the crowds.

8. Be a wildlife detective. If you're not seeing any animals look for clues, such as tracks, scats, nests, or burrows. Finding this evidence of wildlife can be every bit as fulfilling as seeing the actual animal—and sometimes even more enlightening. For example, seeing a bear walking won't tell you what it's been feeding on, but poking through its scat will. Also, be aware of the other species. For example, if you're looking for wolves or bears keep an eye out for congregating ravens, crows, vultures, or eagles as they may signal that a kill is nearby.

9. Keep in mind the small things. Is your goal to photograph wildlife? Then you will generally want the sun to your back. Plan your route accordingly. Keep in mind that many animals have an acute sense of smell that they use to detect danger. If you don't want to be detected, move into the wind.

10. Please be careful. Being a cautious wildlife observer will keep you and your loved ones safe and free of injuries. It will also keep the wildlife healthy and alive. This is especially important in national parks where high numbers of park visitors are in close proximity to high numbers of wildlife. Avoid driving too fast, don't expect wild animals to move safely out of the way, and keep a safe

A spotting scope allows great views of wildlife while not disrupting their natural behaviors. (Photo by Gary W. Vequist)

distance from the vehicle ahead of you as it may suddenly stop to view wildlife.

Wildlife-Viewing Ethics

The term *wildlife viewing* is in some ways misleading, as a more precise term could be *wildlife interacting*. Every visitor to a national park who watches wildlife becomes part of the event he or she is observing, and unfortunately, a person can sometimes become part of the event in undesirable, harmful, and even fatal ways. The wildlife watcher who keeps the parent birds away from a nest, a turtle hatchling from reaching the water, or an animal from resting in the shade can cause the death of that animal.

No ethical wildlife observer would want to cause such harm. And wildlife viewing in national parks comes with additional responsibilities. One harmful action by one inconsiderate observer could affect everyone else. For example, if an observer gets too close to a den and causes the adults to abandon the site the park may in the future prohibit access to such areas.

Having said that, we've identified ten codes of conduct for wildlife observers (yes, another list). They are:

1. View from a distance. Viewing wildlife from afar minimizes disturbance. And view quietly and with minimal movement and commotion. If you suspect that the animal may be getting nervous because of your presence, you are probably right. Depending on the circumstances try to stay still or back away.

2. Keep on roads and trails. Animals are more tolerant of people on established roads and trails. And you will do less damage to sensitive natural resources. If you must leave the road or trail avoid damage to stream banks, young vegetation, and other ecologically sensitive areas.

3. Never feed wildlife. Never feed wildlife or try to entice its members in any way (e.g., by using calls). Similarly, keep your food secure and out of reach of animals. Animals that associate people with food could end up dead because of it.

4. Control your pets. Generally speaking, pets are of no benefit when viewing wildlife and can lead to problems; if you must have them along, keep them on a leash. Even that apparently "harmless" chasing of wildlife can lead to injuries or mortalities for wildlife.

5. Don't touch or handle injured, weak, or baby animals. You may only make the situation worse. For example, if you touch baby animals the mother may not return to care for them. Also, animals can carry diseases that can be passed to humans, so for your own safety *do not touch.*

6. Avoid unsafe situations. Never get between an adult animal and its young, a predator and its kill, animals during the breeding season, or between groups of animals, especially herding animals.

7. Pick up your trash. Leaving trash is not only unsightly and against the law, the remains could kill animals that try to eat it or get entangled.

8. Leave natural objects where you find them. It may be tempting to bring that feather, bone, or antler home, but you deprive others of the opportunity to experience it. Also, it's against the law to take such items from national park units.

9. Respect others. In parks a wildlife sighting can often lead to a "bear jam" (pick your species; in Africa they have "giraffe-ic jams"). Try and minimize congestion. Never stop vehicles on the road to view wildlife, but rather pull to the side far enough that your wheels are out of the traffic lane (but not so far that you're damaging vegetation). Be careful getting out of the vehicle and watch out for traffic. Don't stand on the road to view wildlife, rather walk to the shoulder. Viewing in small groups is usually less disturbing to wildlife and a better experience for the people. Best to always use soft voices so as not to disturb the wildlife, also to better hear the animals. The cardinal rule: be considerate of others, as you would want them to be considerate of you.

10. Teach others wildlife-viewing ethics. When necessary, diplomatically tell others to do the right thing. Rangers can't be everywhere, so it's up to you as an experienced wildlife observer to help your fellow visitor. Many people simply don't know right from wrong, so if you politely explain why something is wrong they may cooperate. In the worst-case scenario, if they are doing something wrong report the incident.

A bear cub in a tree is cute, but it also makes for an unsafe situation as the mother may be nearby. (Photo by Daniel S. Licht)

Fifty Wildlife-Viewing Destinations

Any "best" list is, of course, built from arbitrary criteria, fraught with personal experiences and biases, and open to debate. Truth be told, the "best" park to view wildlife in is the one you're at, or heading to, as every park has its own fauna, habitats, and scenery. Having said that, in our opinion these are the "Best Fifty Parks for Viewing Wildlife" (table 15). We've also listed a featured species at the parks. How did we select these parks and these species? We chose scenic locations where interesting and appealing creatures are relatively common and readily viewable. Although we personally find that banana slugs meet those criteria, we recognize that most people would rather see bears, wolves, and other "charismatic" species, so our list emphasizes such species. At the same time we tried to cover the breadth of wildlife diversity found in our national parks. We also selected destinations distributed across the United States, with several close to major metropolitan areas.

Table 15. Best fifty parks for watching wildlife

Park	Focal Species	Closest City
ALASKA		
Denali NP	Dall Sheep	Fairbanks, AK
Katmai NP	Brown Bear	Anchorage, AK
Kenai Fjords NP	Orca	Anchorage, AK
ARIZONA		
Grand Canyon NP	California Condor	Phoenix, AZ
Petrified Forest NP	Pronghorn Antelope	Albuquerque, NM
ARKANSAS		
Buffalo NR	Elk	Little Rock, AR
CALIFORNIA		
Channel Islands NP	Elephant Seal	Los Angeles, CA
Point Reyes NS	Gray Whale	San Francisco, CA
COLORADO		
Rocky Mountain NP	Bighorn Sheep	Denver, CO
FLORIDA		
Big Cypress NPres	Anhinga	Tampa, FL
Canaveral NS	Manatee	Orlando, FL
Dry Tortugas NP	Sea Turtle	Key West, FL
Everglades NP	Alligator	Miami, FL

Park	Focal Species	Closest City
GEORGIA		
Chattahoochee NRA	Canada Goose	Atlanta, GA
IDAHO		
Craters of the Moon NM	Short-Horned Lizard	Boise, ID
INDIANA		
Indiana Dunes NL	Sandhill Crane	Chicago, IL
IOWA		
Effigy Mounds NM	Eagle, Hawk, and Vulture	Des Moines, IA
KANSAS		
Tallgrass Prairie NPres	Prairie Chicken	Kansas City, KS
MAINE		
Acadia NP	Harbor Seal	Bangor, ME
MARYLAND		
Assateague Island NS	Horseshoe Crab	Newark, NJ
MASSACHUSETTS		
Cape Code NS	Humpback Whale	Boston, MA
MICHIGAN		
Sleeping Bear Dunes NL	Trumpeter Swan	Detroit, MI
MINNESOTA		
Mississippi NRA	Bald Eagle	Minneapolis, MN
Voyageurs NP	Osprey	Duluth, MN

Park	Focal Species	Closest City
MISSISSIPPI		
Gulf Islands NS	Brown Pelican	Pensacola, FL
MISSOURI		
Ozarks NSR	Wild Turkey	St. Louis, MO
MONTANA		
Glacier NP	Mountain Goat	Spokane, WA
NEBRASKA		
Niobrara NSR	Soft-Shelled Turtle	Omaha, NE
NEVADA		
Great Basin NP	Coyote	Salt Lake City, UT
NEW MEXICO		
Carlsbad Caverns NP	Brazilian Free-Tailed Bat	El Paso, TX
NEW YORK		
Fire Island NS	Laughing Gull	New York, NY
NORTH CAROLINA		
Cape Hatteras NS	Black Skimmer	Norfolk, VA
NORTH DAKOTA		
Theodore Roosevelt NP	Bison	Bismarck, ND
OHIO		
Cuyahoga Valley NP	Beaver	Cleveland, OH
OREGON		
Crater Lake NP	Clark's Nutcracker	Portland, OR

Park	Focal Species	Closest City
PENNSYLVANIA		
Delaware Water Gap NRA	Great Blue Heron	Philadelphia, PA
SOUTH CAROLINA		
Congaree NP	Pileated Woodpecker	Columbia, SC
SOUTH DAKOTA		
Wind Cave NP	Black-Footed Ferret	Rapid City, SD
Badlands NP	Prairie Dog	Rapid City, SD
TENNESSEE		
Great Smoky Mountains NP	Black Bear	Knoxville, TN
TEXAS		
Big Bend NP	Roadrunner	San Antonio, TX
Padre Island NS	Royal Tern	Corpus Christi, TX
UTAH		
Zion NP	Ringtail	St. George, UT
VIRGINIA		
Shenandoah NP	White-Tailed Deer	Washington, DC
WASHINGTON		
Mount Rainier NP	Pika	Tacoma, WA
Olympic NP	Pacific Salmon	Seattle, WA
WEST VIRGINIA		
New River Gorge NSR	Peregrine Falcon	Charlestown, WV

WISCONSIN		
St. Croix NSR	River Otter	St. Paul, MN
WYOMING		
Grand Teton NP	Moose	Idaho Falls, ID
Yellowstone NP	Gray Wolf	Billings, MT

Note: Abbreviations: NP: National Park, NR: National River, NSR: National Scenic River, NL: National Lakeshore, NM: National Monument, NS: National Seashore, NPres: National Preserve, and NRA: National Recreation Area.

Acknowledgments and Credits

We've had the pleasure of visiting every park featured in this book, numerous times for most. However, we still had many information gaps that could not have been filled without generous input from the many dedicated rangers, naturalists, interpreters, biologists, and maintenance and administrative employees at the parks. Several non–Park Service folks assisted as well. We explicitly want to express our gratitude to the following individuals: Jessica Pearce, Sam Brenkman, Pat Crain, Patti Happe, Skip Snow, Jeff Kline, Kim Delozier, Kate Falkner, Sarah Allen, Jeff Selleck, T. K. Kaziki, Paul Gleeson, Cat Hoffman, Jon Preston, John Dell'Osso, Jay Glase, Vicki Ozaki, Jim Cheathum, Craig Hayslip, Gordon Dietzman, Paul Brown, Nancy Gray, Sam Hobbs, Brett Seymour, Cynthia Rubio, Ernie Quintana, Sue Mills, Kerry Gunther, Dan Stahler, Jill Medlund, Dave Roemer, Bill Route, Brian Kenner, Neal Wilkins, Barbara Wilson, Pamela Barnes, Chuck Bitting, Lisa Petit, Meg Plona, Kevin Skerl, Bruce Leutscher, Doug Smith, Bill Stiver, Renee West, Natalie Gates, Nancy Duncan, and Sonny Bass. Many other park employees helped us during our visits by answering questions and informing us of the best places to observe wildlife (just like they will for you). Of course the errors and deficiencies in the book, and we're sure there are some, are ours alone.

We also thank the scientists who study park wildlife and share their information, publications, and insight. The complex but sometimes tedious job of collecting scientific data is critical to understanding parks and for making informed management decisions. People like marine mammal biologist Scott Baker, bat researcher Nickolay Hristov, and sea turtle scientist Donna Shaver are examples of such devoted scientists. We also thank all the folks at the University of Idaho Visitor Services Project for the data they collect on park-visitor activities.

We thank Shannon Davies and everyone else at the Texas A&M University Press for their support, encouragement, and suggestions. We also thank the anonymous reviewers whose comments made for a better book.

Finally, and perhaps most importantly, we thank our families for letting us indulge our passion for parks and wildlife. Sometimes they joined us on these efforts and sometimes they let us travel alone, but always they supported us. For that we are grateful.

Additional Reading

Knight, R. L., and K. J. Gutzwiller, eds. *Wildlife and Recreationists: Coexistence through Management and Research.* Washington, DC: Island Press, 1995, 372 pp.

Louv, R. *Last Child in the Woods: Saving Our Children from Nature-Deficit Disorder.* Chapel Hill, NC: Algonquin Books, 2006, 334 pp.

National Park Service. *Management Policies: The Guide to Managing the National Park System.* Washington, DC: National Park Service, US Department of the Interior, 2006, 274 pp.

Sellars, R. W. *Preserving Nature in National Parks: A History.* New Haven, CT: Yale University Press, 1997, 380 pp.

Index